CONFIDENT MUSIC
PERFORMANCE

CONFIDENT MUSIC
PERFORMANCE
The Art of Preparing

**Barbara
Schneiderman**

AN AUTHORS GUILD BACKINPRINT.COM
EDITION

Confident Music Performance
The Art of Preparing

AN AUTHORS GUILD BACKINPRINT.COM EDITION
Published by iUniverse, Inc.

For information address:
iUniverse
1663 Liberty Drive
Bloomington, IN 47403
www.iuniverse.com
1-800-Authors (1-800-288-4677)

Originally published by MMB Music, Inc.

ISBN: 978-0-595-53132-5

Printed in the United States of America

For my Mother and in memory of my Father,

who inspired my love of music and

made my life of music possible

and in memory of

Victoria Danin and Sidney Foster,

early teachers who were models of humanity

TABLE OF CONTENTS

Guidance Needed for Musicians; A Constructive Program Woven into the
Study of the Music; To Build a Body of Shared Knowledge; Growing
Library; A New Perspective; Music and Science; Finding the E;
Performance Anxiety; Healthy Excitement; Value of Self Esteem in
Performer; Teacher's Opportunity; Effect of Inadequate Preparation;
Anticipate Higher Excitement Level and Develop Performance Strategy

THE PREPARATION PROCESS

Why Music?; "The Magic;" Historic Role of Performer in Creative Process;
Communication with Composer; Performance as Giving; Steeped in
Nourishing Philosophy; Practice Moments of Peace; Varied Responses to
Performance; Affirmative Goals; Quality Survives Human Error; Be Well-
prepared and Savor the Giving; Ardent Commitment; Sincerity and
Quality; Realistic Setting and Repertoire

Journal and Nature Symbols; Heightened Awareness; Inner Life; You are
the Tapestry; Bits of Life to Save and Savor; Imaginary Dialogues; A
Portrait in Words; Personal History; Looking into the Past; What Art Does
For Us; The Power of Music; Reason and Fantasy; Symbolizing and Fluidity;
An Image Completed; How It Works; Aesthetic Order; Movement and
Change in Art and Life; Being "Moved;" A Subtle Process; Walking with
Nature; Earth

Intimate Knowledge of Structure and Specifics; One Performs the Way
One Practices; Integration of All Elements at Each Stage of Study—
Conscious and Unconscious; What is a Musical Idea?; Levels of Analysis;
"Re-Composing;" Determine and Mark Articulation of Ideas; Study Musical
Ideas and Their Realization; Punctuation and Enunciation; Examples of
Elements to Analyze: Melody; Rhythm; Harmony; Texture; Physical Thrust

and Energy; Function, the Affinity of Musical Ideas for Each Other; Character-Sensing; Stimulate Intuitive Responses; Entering the Emotional Current

The Business-Like Stage; Scholarly Attention to the Score; How Much Analysis for Young Children?; Sensory Learning; Nuts and Bolts; Seeds for a Way of Thinking About Music; First Goals of Score Study: Right Notes, Rhythm, Phrasing, Good Fingering; Separate and Develop Skills; Repetition: Enjoying, Evaluating and Improving; Slowly and Steadily; Stopping to Correct; Larger Sections with Separate Hands on Piano; Voice Integrity; Value of Left Hand Study; Establish Geographic Units in Mind Early; Internalize Music Soon; Integrating Skills—The Full Shape of the Music; Analogy to Painting; Descriptive Mode

Structure: Relationships of Musical Ideas; "Paragraphs;" Formal Scheme; Unique Structures—Conventional Expectations and Idiosyncratic Choices; Value of Studying Form; Principles of Composition; Tension and Release—the Primary Flux; Catharsis from Parallels to Ebb and Flow of Life; Refining and Polishing; Alternate Inner Ear with Actual Playing; Personal Imagery and Concentration

Historical Epoch; Judgement and Taste; Intuition and Personality; Pacing, Phrasing and Volume; Study Music for Other Instruments; Interpretative Ideas; Elusive Passages

System of Starting Points; Memorize Points in Logical Formal Groupings; Learning to Use Starting Points—a Reliable Strategy for Performance; Instantly Resume Flow After Any Lapse; Children Learn to "Stay in the Story;" Preserving Mood; Vulnerability and Competence; Calm, Professional Behavior; Rehearse Starting Point System with Gradually Larger Groups; Support System Reassures Performer, Avoids Fear of Failing; Meaningful Patterns Unify and Simplify Memorizing Process; Maintaining Continuity During a Lapse; Improvisation; Letting It Happen; Why It Sounds Like Music; More Launching Pads; Importance of Dissonance; Winds, Strings and Singers; Adventure

How I Feel During Performance; Immersion and Surrender; Intensification and Spontaneity; Vision; Profound Absorption; With an Audience; Comparison with Analytic Phase; The Intermediary Ground; Clues to Your Own Process; Dialogue with Your Critic; Letting Go and Control; Attitude Toward Performance Can Evolve; A Protective Cocoon; To Reverse a History of Performance Anxiety; Perform Only Well-

Ripened Pieces; Anticipation and Control Reduce Stress; Practical Realities of Performance Situations

Tactile Interwoven with Other Learning Modes; Unity and Spontaneity of Body Action; Freedom of Movement; Awareness of Muscle State; Transition to Repertoire; Flexibility Precedes Virtuosity; Imagery Helps the Release; Sensitivity of Touch; An Extension of Your Body; Interplay; Body Position; Total Body Balance; Relating to Your Instrument—Size, Shape, Nature; Friendship; Piano; Voice—You Are the Instrument; Strings; Winds; Efficiency; Inventive Solutions for Knotty Passages; Technique Depends on the Ear; Solving Passage Problems; Understand the Nature of the Challenge; Many Methods; Body Wellness Affects Self-Image

Body Oneness with the Music; Interpretation Enhanced; Emotional Catharsis; Greater Physical Ease; Gertrude Knight—"Your Own Way of Moving;" A Pivotal Evening; Getting Started; A Warm-Up Experiment; Follow Only Deepest Impulses; Moods; Intensifies Perception; Different Receiving Centers; A Serene Approach; Other Starters Stem from Imagery; Spaces Among People; Spatial Compositions; Aesthetic and Psychological Rewards; Intent and Perception; Therapy and Art

Avoid Last Minute Changes; Innovations and Variants; Reviewing Known Piece for Performance; Conducive Environment; Teachers and Confident Performance

CONCLUSION

Cultivate Rich Inner Life—Enjoy Giving; Value Your Uniqueness; Sense of Wholeness Enhances Concentration; Develop all Parts to Initiate Constructive Cycle; The Mind—Central Processor; Plans for Now and Future; Persistence; Integration

ACKNOWLEDGEMENTS

To thank adequately all the people—family, friends, students, colleagues, teachers—who inspired and encouraged the fruition of this book is impossible. I am most grateful to all of them. My parents' role was paramount as I noted in my dedication, as were the gratitude and affection I felt for Sidney Foster and Victoria Danin—early teachers who keenly influenced my outlook, both musical and philosophic. My mother's personal strength and character to this day provide a radiant model; my father's musicality and gentleness were gifts that touched me deeply.

Sidney was not reluctant to discuss antecedent/consequent phrase structure with a child. I remember now with considerable interest how this basic concept stirred me enormously—opening what seemed a wonderland, a compelling, new realm of ideas about music. Vicky, who spoke fluent and musical Russian, introduced me to the breadth of piano literature and the sensitive crafting of every detail. Her warmth, honesty and humor nourished my adolescent years and remain vivid today.

****

"Mrs." Maguire was my first teacher and I loved my walks from school to her house each afternoon. Her parlor and her demeanor had an old-world charm that delighted me. She called me her bubbling-brook and took me to the opera. Because she communicated pleasure in teaching, I felt immediately the magic that music has continued to hold for me.

It was at Harvard that composer Allen Sapp taught me to analyze music with a graphic sense of dramatic function and an eclectic imagery. His intellectual excitement was infectious and his way of thinking about music has been a major factor in my development. During those formative years Norma Bertolami Sapp was similarly pivotal in shaping my pianism. She conveyed with equal dynamism an understanding of pianistic styles and the power of the Vengerova technique. I feel enduring gratitude for both of them.

A year of twentieth century harmony with Walter Piston was a landmark. In his class we created short works in the dialects of composers we were studying. His encouragement and belief in my musicianship inspired me and his wish that I go to France to study with Nadia Boulanger dwells on some fair horizon of my mind as one of Robert Frost's "paths not taken."

I feel thanks for the fine instruction and heartening words of Horazio Frugoni, with whom I studied at Eastman, and Pearl Turner Hoy in California, who provided many opportunities for me to perform and enthusiastically refused to take "no" for an answer.

Adolph Baller, both gracious and intense, could transmit his strong musicality to a student with spontaneous flair in the very moment of music-making. I learned from him how to pedal my Bach tastefully. I recall one day completing the final cadence of the lyrical F sharp Prelude from the first volume of the *Well-Tempered Clavier* when he approached the piano, carrying the open book in both hands. "Why not take a little pedal?" he began with a smile.

In London I had the great pleasure of studying criticism with Felix Aprahamian and piano with Gordon Green. Aprahamian conveyed with nuance an appreciation of both music and the English language. Buoyed by his comments, I would select with delight from a shining array of concert artists, research the program avidly, venture out to the hall, listen with new ears, take notes and write reviews. Green was a devoted teacher who deftly combined nurture with scholarship. He would work conscientiously on detailed interpretation and yet leave room for a student's personal style to develop. I recall warmly the refreshment of joining his wife for tea, good conversation and her fresh-baked lemon cake in the middle of a long afternoon's session.

From Edith Oppens, in a brief but concentrated course at Aspen, I learned critical elements of performance practice and effective study techniques. Oppens' vibrant personality, humanity and knowledge of music history left an indelible impression and her appreciation of my work was important to me.

I am grateful to Aube Tzerko for sharing with brilliance his organic sense of musical structure. To study with Tzerko is to enter his thought process—to experience the ongoing renewal of his conception of the piece at hand, to partake of his fierce fascination with music and his love of it. He transmits the distinguished heritage of his study with Artur Schnabel. Tzerko's ideas and energy imparted a new momentum to my own process.

Warmest thanks to my friends and colleagues who kindly read the manuscript at various stages in its birthing and offered essential encouragement and advice: Mike Senturia, Oliver Sacks, Luise Vosgerchian, Robert Silverman, Frank Wilson, Norm Goldberg, Kyle Pruett, Janet Lamborghini, Theda and Oscar Firschein, Marianna and Bill Goodheart, Kathy and Tom Parker, Nancy and Tom Fiene, Donna Plasket.

I cannot thank my husband Larry enough. A writer himself, his understanding of the process and his steadfast strength have helped me distinctively throughout the years. I want to include appreciation of my sister Anita for the warmth and constancy of her long-distance support. And finally, I am grateful to my children Rob, Claudia, Heidi and Tanya, who have taught me so much by opening up for me their new worlds and their fresh views.

FOREWORD

S tage fright, performance anxiety, jitters, and butterflies refer with varying degrees of directness to the conspicuous ease with which musicians, dancers, public speakers and athletes—all performers, really—collapse into a state of witless, trembling despair at the sight of an audience.

Barbara Schneiderman, pianist, teacher, and humanist, believes that all musicians can and should share their music with others warmly, lovingly and unreservedly. Possessed of a wonderfully empathic feeling for all artists, her ambition is to emancipate those for whom the moment of musical communion approaches in the costume of confrontation.

Her approach is both pragmatic and poetic, because she is that way herself. She shuns fixes of all kinds (especially pills, pep-talks, and panaceas), offering instead a rational and eminently workable program of personal exploration and discovery to be embraced along with the nuts and bolts of musical study, beginning today. In so doing, she joins and reinforces a growing number of teachers and health practitioners offering this advice: that a healthy attitude toward performance is a skill which can be learned, and which will be handsomely rewarded. Confident performance is not a fluke, but the product of imaginative and consistent synthesis of technical and emotional work. It is the musician willing to work for the spiritual vitality of performance skills who will gain full command of his or her own expressive potential. And Schneiderman does not simply exhort; she shows how it is done.

A great deal has been written on this subject, and most of what one finds in articles, scientific papers and books is both illuminating and useful. This book is equal to the best of that tradition, and provides any interested performer with a host of preventative ideas and strategies which are original, practical and extremely valuable. This is a book that merits a place of prominence in your library, but it will not rest there; it will jump into your music bag, hang out on your piano or your bedside table, run off with your friends and not come home until you call it back. Which you will.

Frank R. Wilson

PREFACE

IF YOU ARE:
- a PIANIST, STRING or WIND PLAYER, VOCALIST or any PERFORMER who longs to feel more comfortable performing

- a TEACHER who would like to impart more confidence and security to your students

- a MUSICIAN of any kind who wants to understand more deeply the interactive and fascinating process of studying a piece and preparing it effectively for performance

- a MUSIC LOVER (amateur means "lover of"—forget the usual connotation) who has concluded because of performance worries that music must remain for you a private joy only

- a STUDENT who cares to study music in depth and develop a reliable strategy for performance

- a PARENT who is concerned with your child's musical and emotional development and the role of performance in his life

If you are any of these people, this book may be helpful to you, providing a new way of thinking and working. It describes a complete system of preparation for performance which engages you as a whole person—your mind, your emotions, your imagination, your physique, your aesthetic—and shows how your confidence will be nourished and developed as it is woven into the learning process itself, not appended during the last hours or weeks before performing. Many of the principles will enlighten those who perform in nonmusical situations as well. So much of life involves "performance."

There is an alternative to fluttering fingers and loss of control. It does not lie in last-minute cure-alls or one-dimensional therapies, certainly not in dependency fraught drugs which do not address the roots of the fear or prevent recurrences. Nor, most important, do they provide the long-term self-affirmation and education one needs to build confidence.

Confident performance rests on a solid, broad foundation of skills and attitudes—in the assurance that you know your music thoroughly in detail and structure, that you understand its shape and logic, that you feel a vivid emotional connection with it, that you have a clear and healthy philosophy, that you value the uniqueness of your own artistic and personal contribution, that you have developed a secure physical ease in delivering the composer's message, and most important, that you have a well-rehearsed method for dealing with performance conditions.

This method offers a serenity which allows you to concentrate on distilling the beauty of the music rather than dwelling on fear.

For it is primarily the fear of failing or lapsing that causes the lapses. Once one is assured of a reliable method for managing lapses they rarely occur. We learn to handle those normal passing moments with appropriate calm—maintaining continuity, control and involvement. The development of this skill is as important to the performer as the ability to play the music well.

One can learn not to dissipate creative energy in worry and self-focus, but to direct that force toward the job of making music. The very same human vulnerability that may translate into fear can be honed into sensitive interpretation, into the spontaneity and warmth that communicates to an audience.

This program will help you to appreciate the importance for confident performance of your self-esteem, your attitude toward the music, toward your instrument, toward the act of performing, toward the audience, toward the composer by offering a constructive way of thinking through these issues.

You may feel a new self-validation from awareness of your vital role as a performing artist in our civilization. The performer is a living link in the creative process—breathing life into pages of music which would remain silent without his* personal commitment. He shares the gift of beauty with an audience in need of the humanizing balance that art brings to our lives, contributing to the composer's effort to express in sound the ineffable realities of the human condition.

You will explore and reflect upon your inner history through journal keeping and discover in nature a touchstone for communion with the artist in you. You may learn to identify deeply with music through dance, experiencing a sense of comfort with the human family that can expand to include all audiences.

You will enjoy the refreshment of contacting your own creative sources, activating them, developing them, taking pleasure in the life of the imagination. Your journey to performing confidence entails growth of personal confidence as

---

* For convenience I use in this book the pronouns he, his, him—not with a masculine connotation, but referring generically to all human beings.

well as all the other facets of preparation. We cannot isolate performance from the rest of the self.

We hope to travel along some paths toward a well-integrated sense of personhood, toward the richest awareness of who you are, what you care about and believe, how you can give to other human beings through your art.

You will learn how to prepare with pleasure over a long period of time during which you befriend the music as you study its basic elements—working them into your mind and spirit as well as into your muscles. You will absorb the sounds of harmonic progressions in depth as you linger over their particular beauties, explore the fine turns of a melody, recreate rhythms with character—seeking your own personal route to understanding the dynamic energy, the physical presence of each musical idea, the mood and personality of each thought and its role in the total design of the piece.

You will discover that it is essential and yet not enough to know the music well. You need also *to learn how to perform*; to recognize that you *may* feel differently during performance and that there is a workable system for dealing with these feelings and indeed transforming them so that they do not inhibit your ability to communicate. As you experience the reassuring comfort of the system, the nature of your feelings evolves and it becomes easier and easier to perform.

I have not always been comfortable performing but I enjoy it now. I have known what it is like to have the impulse to give to an audience, the powerful feeling for and understanding of the music without knowing how to deal with performance conditions and one's emotions. I have learned that that knowledge and preparation are essential.

I would like to share with you what I have learned with experience through the years—grinding, painfully at times, through each pitfall, coming up with solutions for the next time, gradually working out a complete healthy process and learning how to guide my students through this program. You may discover one, two or several areas you might develop that will make a major difference for you.

I speak occasionally as a pianist but mostly as a musician, performer and teacher. I would venture that at least 95% of the book will be relevant to any musician.

A significant part of the process involves very careful analysis of the musical ideas—what I like to call "recomposing." I enjoy digging into the music—getting to know its fine details, exploring deeper and deeper layers of meaning, discovering my own connections and associations and working at how best to realize and project the ideas. We need this bed-rock knowledge of musical events to build a reliable interpretation. It must be a felt knowledge as well as an intellectual one, meaningfully anchored in personal imagery and sensitive listening.

Such analysis will not be experienced as a dry academic exercise but as an exciting activity concerned with the physical reality of sounds and their implications for performance—how they move, grow and change; how they make us feel and how to communicate this energy effectively to our audience.

Performance anxiety is so accepted today as a given in our society that the nervous performer image is constantly stereotyped and reinforced in our popular culture—the daily newspaper cartoons, for example.

But the fact is that it does not have to be this way. Let us take a logical and systematic look at what you can do to provide for yourself the ease of mind that will lead to more fulfillment in performance as well as more pleasure in music.

Confidence will be deeply rooted in musical facts, supported by a well-practiced performance strategy, energized by your own artistic resources, secured by a sure physical control and buoyed by an affirming strength of spirit.

INTRODUCTION

CHAPTER I

INTRODUCTION

THE ART OF PREPARING: A HARMONY OF PERSONAL RESOURCES

Guidance needed for Musicians

F lying home in the Summer of 1984 from the Denver conference, The Biology of Music Making[1], I felt an urgency to speed the gestation of this book, long hatching in my mind. That historic forum had been highly successful, stimulating and productive, followed by an equally excellent sequel in 1987, Music and Child Development[2]. Music educators and performers with a high regard for science had joined with researchers and clinicians who value music in a healthy cross-fertilization of thoughts on the physical and emotional needs of musicians, the nature and functioning of the musician's life.

Performance anxiety was a recurrent topic, analyzed in detail but somehow elusive, although therapies were described and demonstrated. It was clear that it is a widespread, serious problem and that guidance is needed. The suffering is real; the gift of artists to society is invaluable.

A Constructive Program Woven into the Study of the Music

Much enlightening and pioneering work was presented—an impressive array of fine minds had been gathered by San Francisco neurologist Frank R. Wilson who deserves highest acclaim for his contributions to the synthesis of science and music.

I emerged from the lectures and discussions with renewed conviction that what we most need to provide is a complete *constructive* and *preventive* program of performance preparation, not to be relegated to the last hours or days or weeks before a performance, but deeply woven into the learning process, months and even years earlier; not reactive or symptomatic treatment but a long-term, well-integrated process that readies students and professionals thoroughly for the experience of performance, both its rigors *and its joys*. We must not assume severe stress as a given in performance.

---

[1] Roehmann, F.L., and Wilson, F. (Eds.) 1988. *The Biology of Music Making: Proceedings of the 1984 Denver Conference.* St. Louis: MMB Music, Inc.

[2] Wilson, F., and Roehmann, F.L. 1990. *Music and Child Development: Proceedings of the 1987 Denver Conference.* St. Louis: MMB Music, Inc.

A total design should unite all the basic areas:

1. Cognitive preparedness, *built into the study of the works to be performed*—enlivened by imaginative interpretation and emotional engagement;
2. Psychological readiness, with an understanding of performance conditions and *an effective system for dealing with them;*
3. An enriched philosophic framework with ongoing personal and artistic development, maintaining a healthy sense of self-worth;
4. Physical mastery with technical proficiency based on flexibility, freedom of movement, and a fluid, comfortable relationship with one's instrument; and
5. Awareness of the practical realities and mechanics of the whole experience which will be largely blended in throughout the entire system. Obviously these areas all overlap and interact and are separated only for orderly discussion and clear understanding. Each pillar of preparation is vital; any one omitted could weaken the structure.

To Build a Body of Shared Knowledge

Those who perform or train musicians to share their skills and feelings with pleasure can be helpful to other teachers, music-lovers and performers by describing their methods and experiences. It is in this spirit that I offer the results of over forty years of piano teaching and performance plus two recent years in the role of cello student, where I gained invaluable insights into the learning process from the other chair and with a new instrument. Let us build a body of shared knowledge to help young artists develop with confidence and satisfaction and avoid the emotional difficulties some of us have experienced at some time in the past.

Growing library

Recently I dipped with pleasure into the small but growing library of books on music performance, an exploration postponed until I had finished my own foray. There I discovered an exhilarating confirmation of my thoughts, a host of stimulating ideas and the reassurance that my book brings a new dimension to the discussion.

It is comforting to know that helpful information is out there for musicians in a variety of domains. A visit to the library or bookstore will prove rewarding. Also during the last decades a number of conferences have been held, clinics and journals established.[1] Scientists are becoming increasingly interested in how

---

[1] Bibliography available from the International Arts-Medicine Association, 19 South 22nd Street, Philadelphia, PA 19103.

musicians function and performers have begun to articulate their views on these issues more fully.

In 1973, violinist Kato Havas offered a thoughtful and concentrated appraisal in *Stage Fright, Its Causes and Cures, With Special Reference to Violin Playing*—a source of insightful pedagogy and practical studies (Havas 1973). An imaginative contribution was made by teacher and pianist Eloise Ristad with *A Soprano on Her Head, Right-side up reflections on life and other performances*, a book I have long owned but just now read thoroughly (Ristad 1982). As the jaunty title suggests, Ristad employs humor to great advantage as she leads us to outwit our inhibitions but there is a resonant depth to the flip side of the fun. In a lively workshop at the Denver Conference she demonstrated the effectiveness of her awareness techniques. Her passing is a tragic loss to all of us.

The following year Robert Triplett developed a probing psychological portrayal in conjunction with whole body exercises in *Stage Fright, Letting It Work for You* (Triplett 1983). In 1984, Robert Woolfolk and Paul Lehrer edited and contributed fine scholarly analysis to *Principles and Practice of Stress Management*, a highly enlightening spectrum of essays on stress reduction and relaxation methods from Yoga to cognitive therapy (Woolfolk and Lehrer 1984). Professor Lehrer also spoke in Denver on clinical research contributions to the field, pointing out that there were then "fewer than a dozen published parametric studies."[1]

Pianist Dale Reubart combined performing and teaching experience with keen perception in *Anxiety and Musical Performance; On Playing the Piano from Memory*. (Reubart 1985). This articulate inquiry appeared in 1985 and offered much basic advice along with a survey of relevant therapies. Frank Wilson in 1986 made a unique case for the proposition that we humans are remarkably well-suited for making music in his disarming book *Tone Deaf and All Thumbs? An Invitation to Music-Making for Late Bloomers and Non-Prodigies* (Wilson 1986). He conveys in a conversational style a great amount of biologic science useful to musicians. Several comments are quoted herein.

Also in 1986 (the pace quickens) Barry Green, bassist and teacher, wrote with W. Timothy Gallwey *The Inner Game of Music*, applying to music, principles of learning Gallwey had derived from tennis and skiing (Green and Gallwey 1986). The theory is presented in direct, appealing language along with specific teaching techniques and exercises geared to reduce mental interference with one's full potential.

---

[1] Published as: Research on the causes and cures of performance anxiety: A review. In *The Biology of Music Making: Proceedings of the 1984 Denver Conference*, edited by F.L. Roehmann and F. Wilson, 32-46. St. Louis: MMB Music, Inc., 1988.

While far from a complete listing, these references may provide for the reader a variety of paths into our subject and some sense of its history. (This is an experiential book, not a research document.) It is pertinent to my way of thinking that several of the titles include the terms stage fright and anxiety. I chose instead to write a book about confidence. That may begin to differentiate my offering which attempts to build strength from within and from the outset rather than treat symptoms—a constructive, preventive approach dwelling in the rich material of music, how one may study and understand it.

It *is* possible to perform comfortably. I present, as I have outlined and will develop in detail, a multifaceted program involving the whole person and built into the very process of learning music, accepting the notion of human fallibility and generating a reliable strategy for performance. Freedom flows from trust in that plan when it is part of a total design.

I have reframed some of the issues in poetic terms as well as in the concrete and ephemeral elements of the musician's craft. I emphasize art itself, not as therapy but as a way of living. I suggest avenues toward a full inner life, a necessary solid core of personal strength—ways of weaving a meaningful fabric of one's life so sturdy strands will connect us to the music. We examine what art does for us, how we can give and grow through this eminently civilizing process.

The performer's state of mind is a distillation of his everyday experiences. Perhaps we can prevent erosion of one's inherent will by such rootedness in the "music" of living even as we need to be deeply immersed in the current of the music as we perform.

A New Perspective

I would like to offer renewed hope to those who have suffered with stage fright and concluded that music must remain only a private joy for them. One is constantly in the process of becoming oneself—we are not formed as of this moment for all time. Fresh perceptions may heal those wounds, redirect your path and make musical sharing and communicating a possibility.

Recently, out walking, I was struck by the architectural grace of a middle-aged tree. My eyes continued to gaze at the pattern of its branching limbs while my legs carried me beyond the original perspective to a totally new yet equally striking view. The limbs which had entwined now seemed freer, more spaciously arranged.

"How different it appears from this angle" I thought. "Just a few steps farther down the road and it looks like another tree." My mind leaped to the refreshing analogue with human beings. Yes, with the passage of time one may find a new way of looking at an object or oneself or a problem—light from another angle may create a completely new silhouette or illumine some critical facet of truth. A shift in perspective might even crack a worn, outgrown facade constructed as a defense long years ago.

Music and Science

The informed perspective of music practitioners might also benefit medical clinicians (especially since they counsel musicians) and researchers, both of whom seek fuller understanding of these phenomena. We can all learn from each other as we explore with our own skills and backgrounds the nature of this human experience.

> "As scientific or artistic creators, we do not solve the jigsaw puzzle of reality.
> Rather we build endless realities out of Lego."
> —(Gardner 1982, 62)

Neatly expressed by psychologist Howard Gardner in his outstanding book *Art, Mind and Brain*, this bracing thought reminds us that there is no single answer. We may feel a pressing need to explore this subject and discover more understanding but we ought to proceed with humility, aware that each of us contributes only a "version of the world" (Gardner 1982, 62) which hopefully moves us a little farther down the road. There can be no absolute certainty; there should be no dogma.

Finding the E

John Holt, the eminent educator, told a story about Pablo Casals in his extraordinary book *Never Too Late* (Holt 1978). A friend of Casals observed the cellist practicing a C major scale one morning after sharing the master's daily walk along the beach. Casals played the C, then the D, followed by a lengthy, careful, repeated playing, listening, checking, and verifying the precise placement of his finger on the C string for the exact intonation of E.

Struggling on, the gentle master noticed his friend "staring at him" and explained. "Always, everyday for fifty years, I have to find the E." Holt continues: "Yes. Everyday we have to find the E. It is not a matter of finding it, once and for all, when we begin to play, and then having it forever. We have to keep finding it." (Holt 1978, 199).

And all of us have to keep looking, keep finding, refinding and clarifying our truth even as we do our daily work—open to change, self-examining, always learning, always growing.

Performance Anxiety

Let us clarify before we go on what we mean by performance anxiety. We are not talking about the healthy excitement normally associated with moments of challenge or the brief butterfly that might flutter within at the thought of performance. That welcome and familiar body response cannot and should not be prevented. It is, in fact, a sign of life, of warmth—a function of the same sensitivity that responds to the gentle nuance or the passionate urge of the musical moment.

Performance anxiety refers rather to those symptoms which inhibit the natural expression of emotion and the secure functioning of muscle and memory. The litany is well-known; shaking legs that won't control the pedal, moist fingers that cannot secure the string, a distracted mind that will not focus on the composer's line of thought (all of which may appear with mere anticipation of performing). A fear of faltering in *any* way may become, in worst cases, a fear of fear itself that can worry a performer offstage as well and has caused some to avoid public recital or even change careers.

Healthy Excitement

To amplify our discussion of these two states, one should dwell for a moment on a positive note, on the nature and significance of that normal excitement that should not be repressed but appreciated in context—indeed, it is a quality to be valued as a useful human response to meaningful challenge. Channeling it appropriately prevents it from becoming anxiety.

We can welcome this heightened emotional state for it projects a performer onto the level necessary to feel, to energize, to *recreate* the intensity of the music. To match the fervor of the creative act requires a state of being that rises above the mundane. This special energy will indeed serve the music, but only when a musical offering is supported by a firm foundation—an intimate and thorough knowledge of the music, preparation for the conditions of performance and a sense of harmony within.

Value of Self-Esteem in Performer

This inner peace derived largely from self-esteem is indeed an essential ingredient in performance. Here I would like to emphasize the importance for a performer of a positive self-image and the key role of the music teacher in nourishing that image. Obviously, home environment is central to one's emotional growth and these principles have great relevance for parents as well.

At the 1984 Denver conference pianist Lorin Hollander spoke eloquently of the urgent need today for the arts in education as a humanizing force in a world badly out of tune, and of the opportunity, in this climate, for music teachers to become healers, to nurture self-esteem in students and affirm their finest values.[1] He quoted a Sufi saying: "Look not for the devil in the desert. Look in the overcritical teacher," attributing that "tightening" during performance to one's projection onto an audience of the "critical other" felt within, the scarred residue of wounds inflicted long earlier, when the child in a vulnerable state ventured forth to share and met rejection.

A performer needs to value himself, to feel that he has a message worth sharing, something special to contribute. One gives in performance the gift of oneself. Each of us is unique and inimitable—a blend of all the experiences and influences of a lifetime. You are the only expert on being you. To be yourself, to make contact with the changing, flowing river of your development, to appreciate yourself, is a corollary of the authentic musical experience, both a necessity and a result. Improvement is always possible; one could start rebuilding right now.

Indeed, it is essential for any human being to believe in his personal ability in order to learn or achieve in any capacity. Confidence cannot be swallowed like a vitamin pill or injected as a last-minute counter measure. It must be fed from a deep well of self-esteem that grows gradually over months and years, evolving with beneficial life experiences.

Hollander suggested that teachers need to learn to understand and heal their own "resentments and fears" to become nurturers of healthy-minded students (Hollander 1988, 49-50). That's a huge assignment but it is so important that increasing emotional health be passed along to the next generation rather than perpetuating the flaws of the past. We must all consider this seriously, teachers, parents, teachers-and-parents-to-be.

I believe, paraphrasing a popular current adage, that "you are what you *do*!" Every time we make a choice of how we will spend an hour or a half-hour we are shaping our lives, our selves, our neurons. Whatever the past, we each have the power now in our own hands to improve, to choose those activities that nourish, to self-educate, to tap our creative juices and transform our self-concept.

Teachers' Opportunity to Cultivate Students' Self-Respect

> To teach is to sensitize.
> —(Wiesel 1982)

Every exchange between teacher and student (or parent and child) presents an opportunity to cultivate or diminish self-respect in the student; either to call

---

[1] Published as: The price of stress in education. In The Biology of Music Making: Proceedings of the 1984 Denver Conference, edited by F.L. Roehmann and F. Wilson, 47-51. St. Louis: MMB Music, Inc., 1988.

forth the uniqueness of that individual and help him feel his own strengths and know his own opinions, or set up arbitrary external authorities and snip off the budding artist. For a fine understanding of this essential dynamic, I highly recommend to all Dorothy Corkille Briggs' book *Your Child's Self Esteem* (1975).

The teacher's role is to enable, to encourage an educated independence, not create dependency. The sensitivity that is capable of conveying subtlety in music is delicate. It must be cultivated and nourished to bloom into a finely honed musical sensibility, not truncated or distorted or limited in its development. As John Holt tellingly put it, "we learn through our strengths, not our weaknesses."[1]

Some of us have been exposed, usually at advanced levels, to the harshness and thoughtlessness of people who attempt to teach through intimidation and we have felt the damage. Rather than decry their lack of humanity, ironic in this field of the "humanities," we must recognize sadly that they too have been deprived of nurturing. But even those of us who are more generous in spirit need to be reminded of the powerful influence we exert on our students' emotional development; that a person needs to be led to value himself, his own distinctive combination of traits, his own instincts and intuitions, his own ways of thinking and feeling in order to become a confident, well-balanced performer and human being.

In phrasing comments, one can be sensitive to the tentative blossoming of musical taste, saying, for example, "which way do you prefer?" or "do you like this kind of articulation at the cadence?" And when you want strongly to suggest a particular quality "It seems to me..." is better than "Here you should..." One can encourage and help develop musical judgment and musicianship thus: "Some scholars believe such and such. How does it sound to you this way?"

The teacher is a model for the student's "becoming"—his self-realization. One's tone can convey approval of the person even as you work to improve the passage. One can always find something to praise before proceeding with critical comments. This nurturing approach is emphasized in the Suzuki Method (Suzuki, 1969), which I follow with my young students.

One can stimulate the imagination to evoke a real personal response and emotional identification with the composer's feelings—"What do you feel is the mood of this passage?" "What is the composer trying to say here?" "Which composer do you prefer?...Which piece? Why? How does it make you feel?"

Your student is painting a portrait of himself as reflected by your words and your tone of voice. If you address him respectfully, he will begin to feel self-respect. If you recognize and encourage his personal directions in music, a valid

---

[1]   From Holt Lecture attended by the author in Escondido, California, July 16, 1984.

artistic self and a potent inner life will start to take shape. If your voice expresses affection, he will feel liked and will better like himself.

Furthermore, David Nyberg, Professor of Philosophy of Education at SUNY Buffalo, in his sensitive book *Tough and Tender Learning* (1971), offers that the manner and attitudes of the teacher are being taught even more than the words. There is "inadvertent teaching...happening through the student's perception of the teacher's 'silent language', his feeling, tone, posture, timing and choice of words" (pp. 33-4).

One need not disparage to improve. Indeed, a caring teacher gently leads the way to knowledge with understanding of the total human being involved in this effort; his emotional life, his mental health, his current and future responses to both the challenge of performance and the challenge of life.

Effect of Inadequate Preparation

It is not enough to teach the music well, give some enthusiastic words of encouragement and hope for the best at performance time, leaving to a youngster the burden of managing unexpected emotions and their effect on his rendition of the music. The harm that may ensue can be long lasting.

Some of us are fortunate to have received appropriate instruction for performance. But we all have in our memories various versions of those nightmare moments, both for audience and performer, of the student recitalist stuck in the rut of a misplaced transition, or the right theme in the wrong key, unable to find a way out—either forced to return endlessly to the beginning of the piece or, having faltered and paused, unable to reenter the flow of the music and continue.

Or, in another bleak scenario, a student is tense and physically ineffective, obviously straining under pent-up pressures, his fingers losing their ability to function and merely skittering across the surface of the music. All tone and meaning lost in the tidal wave of emotion, he hardly hears the sounds he is producing, missing notes and even whole passages in an effort to get through somehow and end the nightmare. The restorative power of the artistic experience has been distorted. How long will it take him to recuperate, how is he going to feel about the next performance and what mark will be left upon his psyche?

Many of us have finally learned from these youthful experiences with helpful words of wisdom and kindly support from others plus persistent self-education— navigating through all the rapids to discover and analyze, one by one, how to anticipate, prepare for and avoid them.

But some have continued to carry the baggage of these memories through life, either to scar their love of music and their confidence, to render impossible further attempts at performance, or to set a pattern for a performing career of chronic tension.

Children can be spared this trauma and, indeed, experience the opposite— the character building and rewarding joy of *giving* through performing—if they are prepared appropriately. They can be taught behaviors and attitudes specific to performance in addition to fine musical instruction. The depth of their involvement in music making (personal, imaginative), the attitude toward self, composer and audience, an understanding and acceptance of human fallibility and how to handle lapses calmly are all features which can prepare them and can be taught.

It is not enough to say "Don't be afraid." We can help by stimulating a full, vivid inner world that so occupies the mind that there is no room for fear. We can fill up the imagination with active and creative music making, prepare the mind to understand and control the performance situation, guide the spirit into constructive channels.

Let those of us who are teachers accept the responsibility of caring for the inner lives of our students as well as their musical training by taking a rational approach to this issue, instructing ourselves and them in depth in all aspects of how to study and perform as well as how to play our instruments.

Once you have digested and benefited from this material, you might enjoy passing the ideas along to your college and adult students. Certain adolescents will also respond at this level. I will provide occasional guidelines for younger students as we proceed. Though the principles are universally relevant, children's maturity levels and individual needs vary widely and you will need to decide how to apply the specifics of the program appropriately for each child in language he will understand.

Anticipate Higher Excitement Level and Develop Performance Strategy

We need to acknowledge the real difference between one's state of being during practice and during performance. The subtleties of these differing states are explored in Chapter V. We recognize that there *will* be a higher excitement level and that we must be prepared to handle it. We need to develop a strategy for dealing with lapses. As part of our learning process, we try to create performance excitement and work with it. We learn to concentrate, to resist distraction, to maintain emotional commitment to the music.

We learn to accept and cherish our humanness—we will not be so flawless as the artificially perfected disc or tape, but we have warmth and spontaneity to offer. We know that even the great artists misstep from time to time and we learn, as they do, the controlled professional behavior at those moments that is reassuring both to oneself and one's audience.

The performance strategy begins with, and is ingrained in, our study of the music as we become intimately familiar with sections as structural units, securing an ineradicable knowledge of starting points which act as a support system when we perform—a mental map to carry along through the piece, assuring that you always know exactly where you are and what comes next, developed in Chapters IV and V.

Once a musician discovers through practice performances that he can depend on this system, the security it brings is so reassuring that it is usually not even necessary to call upon it in performance. The increased confidence creates a calm mental state in which one is able to focus energy on one's experience of the music rather than of the self.

THE PREPARATION PROCESS

THE PREPARATION PROCESS
Chapters II-VIII

KNOWLEDGE AND MOTIVATION

In deciding where to begin describing the actual process of preparation, all of the outlined areas are so interdependent and vital that it is difficult to prioritize their importance. We know that the best insurance against performing problems is really knowing the music well, and knowing that you know it, beyond a doubt, so we will deal with cognitive preparation in great detail. Yet no matter how well you know the music objectively, subjective issues are paramount in affecting one's state of mind during performance and motivation provides the critical motor energy for all endeavors. Why you are doing something always affects how you feel about doing it.

So I have chosen to begin with an exploration of the deeper truths, the values involved. We need to secure a philosophic framework first, to deal with motivation and meditate upon the questions: why music? why performance? We each need to ponder and sort out our reasons for performing, to understand the role of performing artist.

A mind filled with realization of the transcendent beauty of music and the renewing gift it offers will be less vulnerable to distraction.

CHAPTER II

SAVOR THE GIVING—PHILOSOPHIC FRAMEWORK

Why Music?

> Life is short and art long...
> —Hippocrates

Since attitude is so closely allied with motivation, it is helpful to think through our rationale for bringing music into our lives. What is the value of music-study from a philosophic point of view?

The following excerpt (pp. 16-20) first appeared as part of an article in the *Journal of the Suzuki Association of the Americas* (Schneiderman 1983). It was originally intended for parents of music students but this edited version might be appropriate for all of us to consider at this point. Perhaps it will refresh our thinking a bit:

What does music do for us? Why seek music for ourselves or our children?

It is difficult to articulate something as subjective as the value of studying music precisely because music is a language that goes beyond words, a voice of the human spirit. In an earlier time, music was regarded as a special, pure state of mind and quality of being. The condition, to be *with music*, was equivalent to virtue. As Cassiodorus, the Sixth Century monk and music theorist, said:

> The discipline of music is diffused through all the actions of our life. First, it is found that if we perform the commandments of the Creator and with pure minds obey the rules he has laid down, every word we speak, every pulsation of our veins, is related by musical rhythms to the powers of harmony. Music indeed is the knowledge of apt modulation. *If we live virtuously, we are constantly proved to be under its discipline, but when we commit injustice we are without music.* (Author's italics)
>
> —(Strunk 1965, 88)

This brings to mind on a more universal level Kepler's sense of awe at the "continuous song" in the laws of planetary motion and Milton's "harmony divine."

How does this extraordinary value, this harmony, express itself?

To begin, while interpreting a piece, one may feel an ascent of consciousness to the artistic level. A musician's awareness grows as he stretches his imagination to understand and fulfill the design of the composer, to feel and know what he felt and knew. There is an expansion of the sense of self through this growing to fill the music, to become equal to it, to enrich it with new life and participate in the creative adventure. The abundant energy of the composer is communicated through the music; the musician absorbs it and is enhanced by it.

In another sense, an elevation of outlook can come from experiencing the nonmaterial values inherent in music; the aesthetic, the transcendent, the pure. It exists not for a reason. It simply is. It is nonfunctional and beautiful. It expresses the sublime, closer perhaps to religion, to spiritual values than to object or quantity. In a materialistic society, the balance music brings is especially beneficial.

A significant element is the emotional growth that derives from exploring the range of moods and characters in musical expression. One's ability to feel, to be sensitive to people, to events, to other art forms, is heightened. A musician comes to know a broad variety of feelings through recreating them in music. His emotional palette is enriched by a wide spectrum of hues and his emotional life is correspondingly brightened, beyond the ordinary possibilities of daily living.

In addition to this breadth of sensitivity, musicians speak of the depth of fulfillment music brings. The opportunity to experience and convey subtle states, nuances that words cannot equal, is the privilege of the musician. The ineffable, the elusive, the intense, the profound, can find expression in artful patterns of sound. When one is stirred by such moments, every cell in the body may feel illumined. A deep catharsis often comes after an important musical experience and even, yes, after practicing!

Indeed, many of us are aware of the magical power of music to transform one's outlook. Something in the sequence of harmonies or the structural logic or the turn of a melody or the flux of the rhythm or a synthesis of all these and other elements seems to be able to restore balance in human beings, to inspire us, to comfort and relax us, to affect us in a most uncanny way. How it happens remains largely mysterious but that it happens is a precious gift of life.

Let us not forget the delight we feel in the aesthetic and sensory pleasure of the experience. Melody, rhythm and harmony combine to form a feast for the ear and thereby the heart.

This activation of one's aesthetic sense will foster a capacity to discover and appreciate beauty wherever it is found, in art, in nature, in life. Familiarity with musical principles of form, design, composition, elemental relationships, the development of ideas, help us understand the other arts as well: literature, painting, sculpture, dance, theater. All the arts share certain aesthetic notions such as balance, proportion, unity, variety. These ideas, absorbed partly through concrete study and partly on an unconscious level, will cultivate a sensitivity to beauty that extends even to viewing a flower or reading a poem or enjoying the harmony of color in a human face.

A musician knows the supreme joy of sharing music with others. Given the intensity of the musical experience with its acute emotional involvement, the personal commitment of energy in devoted preparation, immersion of all in vibrant sound, performance is indeed a gift of the musician to an audience even as it is a lofty moment for himself. The responsiveness of the listeners, heeding the message and grateful for the artist's offering, completes the circle, assuring the performer that he has communicated. He has projected the essence of the composer's will as he perceives it, infused with his own insight and emotion. The spirit of giving one's best to render the beauty of the music and keep the composer's ideas alive is an enlightened attitude for one to take into performance. It de-emphasizes the ego and invokes our finest human qualities—integrity, humility, dignity, benevolence—creating a rare social experience to match the musical.

The cooperation and flexibility required in chamber music provides another healthy social experience. Searching along with other musicians for the heart of the music and expressing it effectively together requires both a commitment to the group as a whole and a hardy individuality, as players dialogue with musical ideas as in conversation. At times one leads, other times one follows and at still other moments, there is equality in the parts. Players pick up interpretive clues from each other and respond in kind, or discuss different renderings based on their intuition, experience or knowledge of the style of the composer or the period.

Similarly in an orchestra there is the joy of cooperating in a shared experience. There may be less room for individual expression and give and take than in chamber music, but there is the unique excitement of many voices joined to form a magnificent whole, larger than the sum of the parts and only possible when each player contributes and understands the grand scheme as the conductor unfolds it. None could do it alone but each is vital to and responsible for the splendor of the total effect.

Indeed, the feeling of achievement that accrues from music learning is of great value to a student's developing sense of self-esteem. (This central issue of self-esteem returns again; it is a universal factor in education and a critical matter for parents and teachers to understand.) The ability to sustain a high level of involvement over many years, with all the ups and downs inherent in any serious pursuit, builds a strong sense of character. Mastering an instrument requires discipline and dedication and rewards a student with the sense of a purposeful, accomplished life as well as all the other joys of music.

Not to forget the most obvious, a musician will develop his physical ability to a highly refined level in the nature of neuromuscular flexibility and control. Strength and coordination are necessary to execute passages of nuance as well as those of vigor. These skills will advance along with the stages of repertoire and he will enjoy a sense of dexterity to match the growing sensitivity.

One's hearing, of course, will grow in refinement. The ability to distinguish delicate detail and shades of tone quality and volume creates a keen alertness and fine-tuning in a musician.

Cognitive ability also evolves through the concentration required in studying music. The powers of mind as well as emotional and physical resources are unified as we learn and mental agility may be enhanced by this comprehensive integration of brain/body skills. Later we will explore the fascinating matter of the relative proportions of reason and feeling involved at various stages of preparation. (Chapters III and V).

Of course with younger children the absorption of material is more direct and intuitive but the mind is undoubtedly active—digesting and assimilating information albeit nonverbal. Increasingly, children will use their conscious mental powers in learning how to study music systematically (a skill that will be beneficial in other pursuits as well). They will be referring actively to previous knowledge as they work on interpretation and they will become more analytic as they seek to understand and memorize longer pieces, consciously noting features such as structure, harmonic modulation, thematic treatment.

In a beautiful sense, there is an enlargement, an enrichment of the self as a person absorbs each new piece of music similar to that phenomenon one feels in memorizing a poem. It becomes part of you, you become part of it—an organic fusion takes place and you are somehow amplified. With the understanding of a great work of art, one grows deeper and richer, one's life fuller. A student may happily think that he now has a bit of Bach or Beethoven within him when he knows a piece well.

In fact, the pleasure of learning itself is another benefit. A student will gather knowledge of the lives of composers, of other instruments, stylistic periods, theory, even some elementary physics as he explores sound production, the harmonic series, sound waves, string vibrations. Such learning may stimulate a desire for more learning—weaving this knowledge of the world into his broader general education.

His understanding of history, in particular, will be enhanced through music by familiarity with the characteristic culture of a period, a country or a people. For example, when it comes to studying 19th Century European ideas, the student who knows "in his bones" the music of Chopin or Beethoven and their life-stories is well-equipped with background. The intimate and specific information of the senses will bring life to his awareness of history.

On a more reflective plane, music can give perspective and breadth to our lives. Creations of art allow relief from the daily preoccupation with survival. Music reaches beyond questions of man's existence even as it intensifies our humanity— life is finite, but music remains. It provides a connection with the past and future. Experiencing the immortal qualities of beauty in the music, we feel a link with eternal values. The music has existed for hundreds of years—it will survive as long as civilization can.

Questions of space and time boggle man's imagination; life is complex and difficult to understand. Man makes designs and patterns in art as he looks for them in history and science, to bring order to life, to please his senses and his mind with this order, to make sense out of the infinite possibilities, the diversity of life. We can see how the study of art is deeply reassuring to people. It endows life with form and value.

Later we delve more into the gift of the artist and the nature of the creative act—how we help each other through art.

"The Magic"

An article by cellist Lynn Harrell on "this marvelous creature, the orchestra" (Harrell 1988) goes to the heart of the question: why music? Here are some excerpts but I recommend the whole remarkable essay.

> ...What has stayed with me—and sustained me—over the years is the magic...the extraordinary memories. James Levine's first time out in Cleveland (a Beethoven Seventh in a kiddies' concert), with precise "Uncle George" [Szell] rushing back after the last movement, horrified at such unbridled vigor and youthful muscle. "What have you done to my orchestra?" he shouted. Exhilarated us, as it happens...
>
> Leonard Bernstein's Mahler Second in the muggy summer heat of Blossom, Ohio; Elizabeth Schwarzkopf rehearsing *Four Last Songs* with Szell as the sunset glimmered on her golden hair—a true twilight of the gods. The passion of Jan Peerce, the brilliance of Marilyn Horne, the spare elegance of Rudolf Firkusny— these were the highlights of my musical education...
>
> I shared these with the colleagues of my soul...my friends, their faces and inner beings driven into my heart in the fire of those great and inspired performances. The heightened intensity, the moments when you play beyond yourself and, as a group, understand as the last note dies that something very special has passed between and fused you. Those are the songs without words, the magic of an orchestra, experiences that defy explanation and logic...playing and rejoicing in

the greatest music written by the greatest composers. I remember how it feels to
be opened this way when you are young...

Historic Role of Performer in Creative Process

Children and adults alike respond to an awakening of their sense of the
historic role of the performing artist in the creative process. It is clear that the
music, unlike a finished painting on a museum wall, would remain mute, locked in
a book and gathering dust on a shelf were it not for your efforts to give it voice.
You contribute your time and thought and caring to the music; you add your vital
energies, emotions and interpretation to the message of the composer, bringing
the music to life.

In addition to the satisfaction of self-expression, the performer thus offers a
service to society and to the composer. This kind of perspective can alter a
limiting and inhibiting orientation to self and displace those disturbing and
destructive questions—"how will I do?" and "what will they think of me?" It moves
the spirit beyond a narrow personal focus on the exigencies of the moment into a
vast panorama of time and a mission of service.

Communication with Composer

We go on to emphasize the performer's communication with the composer.
What an amazing experience to enter through his music the heart and mind of a
great artist who lived hundreds of years ago or lives today. We cross centuries,
continents, cultures and share through this universal language, in a living moment,
that composer's spirit, his selfhood. For music, of all the arts, possibly because of
its many parallels with the basic rhythms of life, the patterns of ebb and flow, has
been likened by Schopenhauer to the very *will* of man. Walter Pater has said, "All
art constantly aspires towards the *condition of music*," (Pater, 1898) its wordless
eloquence and correspondence to life forces. (Author's italics)

This interaction with the composer is an expanding notion and an uplifting
one. It enhances a performer's sense of the significance of the experience and
leads one outside physical limits of body and space to a level of existence above
the material, the temporal, the self-centered. One needs to arrive at this higher
plane not only to avoid certain pitfalls but to do justice to the music and to the
value of the act of recreating great art.

Performance as Giving

Also beneficial to a musician's spirit is the idea of performance as giving. The
artist's offering is a gift not only to the composer and to society in the broader
sense, but to one's particular audience. The gift is enormous—hundreds, perhaps
thousands of hours of study and training beforehand and now, one's own vitality

reaching out to communicate with other human beings in a bonding of artist with audience.

Renewing energy is imparted to the listeners as one projects the mood and tells the story, inviting them closer to the rare qualities of the music, moving, refreshing, bringing new life. Music has a unique power to alter peoples' moods. How invigorating for students and performing artists to be aware of the singular renewal they offer to fellow humans.

The audience is needy, in the sense that they require the balance that art brings into their lives. After a hard day's work, they are there waiting to receive beauty, to accept your gift, not to inflict criticism or demand perfection. We all need contact with aesthetic values to nourish our souls and brighten our days. The performer offers this most precious gift.

A musician will derive strength from such a constructive human perception of his audience, an awareness of this artistic role and the profound contribution he makes thereby. The spirit of giving and caring will guide him, even as we all need to direct ourselves, to touch our own upper limit—to live in our own highest center of energy, as William James says in *The Varieties of Religious Experiences* ([1902] 1985).

Performer Needs to be Steeped in this Nourishing Philosophy

A person preparing for performance, whether independent adult or student, needs to be steeped in this philosophy. These messages cannot be effective as a last minute lecture or pep-talk. To translate into real motivation, they must be absorbed slowly; for a student, they must be communicated from the heart over a long period of time, both verbally and by example. That is, one must not contradict one's message by one's actions. If a teacher believes in these values, she will transfer them successfully to her pupils, presenting them thereby with an invaluable gift.

In order for a nourishing philosophy to become the guiding force, one must not alter one's course for temporary goals such as competitions, exams or auditions, for which we prepare peacefully in the context of our larger goals, adhering to our values. Presented with consistency, the deeper education we are describing will have the lasting positive effect on a student's development as well as providing a healthy perspective from which to view these shorter term events.

Practice Moments of Peace

In practical terms, how do we implant this beneficial attitude? In addition to the personally enriching activities to be described, practicing moments of peace before performing can become a soothing habit, a time of reaching for loftier thoughts, climbing up onto this higher plane as well as centering the body and mind, concentrating on the music, hearing it, enjoying it, entering the mood. For several minutes before and particularly just previous to playing, one should take the time necessary for gathering one's strength, for traveling inward and focusing on these truths.

A teacher can present this activity at lesson time, expect it at relatively informal workshops and recitals in one's home and direct a student to practice these meditative moments regularly at home. Having discussed many times and hopefully modeled the ideas of service, giving and communication, we need to encourage a student to dwell upon these thoughts especially prior to performance, to remain on this high spiritual level during performance, to practice doing it. Emphasize that it is just as important as studying the piece well. When each piece approaches performance level "it is now ready to 'practice performing'; take the time to fill your mind with these good thoughts about music and the gift you give your audience before you play." For some, it is even appropriate to read a page or two of an inspiring book such as Casals' *Joys and Sorrows*, (Kahn 1970) or any poetry, philosophy or biography of similar character.

From the very beginning of study we can encourage an inward gathering of resources, a peaceful focusing on the sound and mood of the music as a student sits at rest prior to playing a song—a Suzuki principle which helps even the youngest child to develop concentration in performance.

During practice performances, we also need to learn to brush away any intrusions immediately, *not allowing them entry*. Instantly sweep away dangerous thoughts like "Gee, things are going well" or "I'm actually feeling pretty good," and return immediately to the center of the music. We can practice this essential technique in protected, "safe" settings until it becomes an automatic behavior, gradually developing the ability to do it in any setting. I remember the actual moment when I taught myself to do this during a performance of a Brahms Rhapsody in Palo Alto, California. I sensed danger and refused to allow it in.

Later, we will develop more completely the idea of practice performing with all the content it requires. Concentration during performance is a central issue. We will see how to build a powerful reality of the music within, including cognitive, emotional, aural and imagistic elements for which one's philosophy serves as matrix.

It is good in general to avoid and deflect any possible causes of tension prior to performance and emphasize peaceful activities—absorbing the beauties of nature, reading, meditating, doing whatever helps you to ascend to a higher plane.

This final peaceful moment of preparation includes an important series of elements of readiness. We want to feel a physical sense of balance and ease throughout the whole body which I call body centering—arms, hands, legs and feet fully at rest, with the torso, supported by the abdominal muscles and strong lower back, resting naturally on the bottom bones. I have heard proponents of the Alexander technique suggest that the spine can grow tall, up and away from the "sit-bones." This action creates an alignment that feels just right, an easy sense of erect posture. We then check our shoulders with a gentle up/down movement to be sure they feel natural and have not climbed upward as the spine lengthened.

Then we center our thoughts. Everyone, from the oldest to the youngest, can close his eyes and travel inward, deeply inward, to find that fountain of his best feelings, his best energies that is inside each of us. Making contact with this powerful personal source, remembering that it is there, is deeply comforting and confirming for a performer.

Next we get our ears and emotions ready. One needs to form a mental model of the music in the "mind's ear" with so much beauty and vitality that one is *eager to begin*, to bring that image to reality. One needs not only to hear the melody, rhythm and harmony of the opening phrase, but to imagine the touch in one's hands, to hear the tone quality, the *tempo,* the dynamic level, to feel the mood with intensity. Then we approach our instrument gracefully (with piano we float up to the keyboard and feel the keys sensitively with a final, natural sensation of flow throughout the arms) and we are ready to enter the music and recreate it with wholeness. The emotional as well as the aural imaging are more developed in Chapter IV and body balance, in Chapters VI and VII.

If this sequence is observed regularly before every piece of music and every practice fragment, each vital step becomes a habit, a mental checkpoint, all eventually telescoped, digested and integrated into a marvelous moment of concentration and repose. When we know and *enjoy* this extraordinary feeling of oneness and comfort and harmony throughout the body, we will be able to reproduce it whenever we need it. The richness of the experience becomes so familiar that I may allude briefly to four steps when I teach—"body centered, thoughts centered, ears ready, feelings ready."

Varied Responses to Performance

Teachers will observe during informal performances when a particular student needs more preparation of the inner self. A studious person who prepares an appropriate piece carefully yet still seems to stumble, and at varying places each time, needs to feel more peace and needs your help in achieving it. Each student has a different temperament, different life experiences and a different nervous system and will require more or less help in each area of preparation depending on the particular emotional and physical realities of their lives. A teacher can be sensitive to the students' responses to performing, observing these individual characteristics and offering appropriate assistance. (Chapter V, etc.)

Affirmative Goals

In contrast with these uplifting ideas, it becomes clear then that setting error-free performance as a goal is both unworthy and distorting. Of course we first do our homework with dedication. We do everything possible in advance to achieve accuracy—indeed, our confidence is directly dependent upon the certain knowledge that we have done just this. We delve into the music thoroughly and in detail, as we will describe, studying it intensively and seriously, giving it our very best effort and determining with good judgment when a work is performance-ready, but we do not go into a recital focused on perfection. In fact, this attitude is kin to an emotional straight-jacket and is likely to produce exactly the opposite effect—tension and blunders.

I would never say to a student "now try to play without mistakes." This plants a negative image, the concentration being on avoidance of error rather than on constructive activity. Better to say, "this time, really feel that driving rhythm" (demonstrating the powerful pulse of the music) or "listen now for a really warm, singing tone" or "feel the darkness, the sadness of the mood in this passage," or, at an earlier stage, "listen for your very best tone on every note." That is, provide an affirmative objective, don't ask for an absence of negatives or errors. Such a stricture amounts to a blight on the spirit and might lead to a terrible fear of the slightest stumble, setting off a chain reaction if it occurs. It focuses a performer's attention exactly where it shouldn't be, on being judged or on judging oneself, rather than on serving the composer's wishes to the best of one's ability, deeply engaged in recreating the mood of the music. Holding out for perfection places your performance in a pressure cooker.

The musician works diligently to achieve a level of understanding and technique equal to the work of art. He then offers the performance from the heart as a gift of his creative energies—not to be criticized in terms of number of errors but to be valued for its genuineness, beauty, sincerity, wholeheartedness.

Quality Survives Human Error

How many of us have been to an error-free professional performance? It is rare. Yet we can be moved, inspired, uplifted just the same. This point must be made clearly, the reality acknowledged. It certainly takes the pressure off.

We're all human together. Doing one's best is all that is ever expected. It is the right notes that count, not the wrong ones.

One of my adult students recently felt a breakthrough in her performing comfort when she assimilated this attitude. She said it had made a tremendous difference for her to understand that one could achieve a very high level of quality, of accomplished playing, and yet embrace this possibility of human error—that the music could tolerate the eventuality of some flaws in presentation and so could she.

Mistakes are a part of life—a well-documented, normal, natural element of human behavior. Why in music-making should people demand of themselves 100% perfection and fear anything less when we know we all continually commit errors in all aspects of daily life, language, for instance.

This point is substantiated in the research of Donald Norman, director of the Institute for Cognitive Science at the University of California, San Diego. He is interested in human memory, attention and action, focusing particularly on human-machine interaction. His distinguished work in effective systems design is based on the assumption of human fallibility—that people, all of us, make errors all the time.[1]

Be Well-Prepared and Savor the Giving

At the moment of presentation, our work is behind us—now we savor the music, the giving, the communication. (With a young student I like to call performance the dessert!) If we believe indeed that we are well-prepared, that we *have* done our homework, an artful rendering is more likely.

We need to know at this moment that we have done our utmost to prepare and that, moreover, we cannot learn the piece *during* performance. It is where it is. Enter the moment, feel the music and you will bring it to life.

With a large dose of modesty one says, "Here I am, I've done my best to study and prepare this great work of art. Now I will enjoy an authentic aesthetic and emotional experience with the music. Its beauty will be communicated best to the audience if *I* am truly rooted in it."

Ardent Commitment

It should be pointed out that there is a healthy version of that compulsive perfectionism. The desire to succeed is natural and welcome in healthy amounts. Along with a positive spirit, it can provide the motor-energy for performance preparation. Furthermore, in some individuals we find a driving desire, even an aesthetic fervor, to achieve artistically, to succeed in recreating the music with grace and vigor. This kind of aspiration, in the context of a well-balanced program

---

[1]   Interview (1988) with Denys Horgan in UCSD Perspectives 1(1):12-15.

of preparation, can function as a catalyst for the strenuous work necessary to prepare thoroughly at a high level. An ardent personal commitment can provide the needed fuel for the demanding physical and mental challenge of performance.

Sincerity and Quality

Another note on the subject of sincerity in performance. I do not mean to equate wholeheartedness with performing success. By itself it is not enough. But when there is quality as well in this gift from the heart we have the makings of a rare moment in the human experience—sincerity then provides the vital ingredient which will be felt and valued by people listening in the audience.

Realistic Setting and Repertoire

It needs to be said also that one should have a realistic comprehension of a setting appropriate to one's level of development. Expectations of finish will vary widely as one progresses from the more casual to more formal situations. But a performer's confidence will grow correspondingly if experiences are positive each step along the way, building a secure attitude. We will later suggest an appropriate sequence of settings. (See Chapter V.)

Also essential is the selection of reasonable repertoire. It is important to be realistic in terms of proficiency level as well as in readiness for understanding style. Since we live with this music over an extended period of time one should also be careful to choose music that will be worthy of continuing study and for which you feel an affinity.

CHAPTER **III**

THE ARTIST WITHIN—PERSONAL ENRICHMENT

At a certain point in [artistic] development, an individual must become self-reflective: he needs to address his own activities, evaluating them in terms of his own goals as well as the values of the culture in which he lives...the opportunity to have diverse experiences and to reflect upon them clearly...may be important in such fields as...music. Possibly the most profound achievements involve the whole person, an individual who has sought to come to grips with himself: only through unsparing self-examination is such deepening likely to come about...the individual must also display staying power: he must have the fiber to transcend an early triumph (or disaster) and continue to deepen.

—(Gardner 1982, 199)

Musical performance occurs at the intersection of three pathways: the historic continuum of art—a wide and generous river indeed, a performing artist's ever-winding road and the life-lanes of listeners in the audience who need art to provide nourishment, restoration and balance on their journeys (all of us at one time or another). We treat the respectful allegiance to the art work itself in Chapter IV as we develop our basic process of study. As for the artist-performer, the richer his inner life, the more fully integrated his personality, the more humane his perspective and whole his world view, the more connections will be made with the music and the more there will be to say to the audience.

Journal and Nature Symbols

Here we explore two ways to develop this wholeness and fullness within, journal-keeping and sensitivity to the symbols of nature. The will to give is another vital component, closely tied to one's feelings about other people. We touch on this here too, but the segment on dance is most pertinent to that particular domain.

Clearly there are many sources of personal enrichment: for one, the exploration of music itself and the other arts—a process of self-discovery as one finds parts of oneself reflected in each phrase, each piece, each composer, painting, poem, film or play one comes to know. Also invigorating are reading, reflection, conversation, study, helping others, creating new things, working in the earth, satisfying work of any kind, museum visits, lectures, etc.

There is a special benefit in pursuits which are active, original and searching within. Deriving from the self and exploring the self, they can increase inner clarity while putting you in touch with your own creativity.

Heightened Awareness

The unique values of the journal—recording your thoughts and observations with the written word—are a heightened awareness of feelings and events in one's life and a deepening of perceptions. You develop a finer sensitivity to moments in time, to everyday happenings, noticing more and considering more your inward responses—to friends, passages, birds, breezes, words, children.

> Del Mar 1973
>
> Tanya, quietly kneeling for a very long time on the ground, closely observing a bright butterfly freshly born from his cocoon...she watches it climb out, sees it sitting on a flower drying in the sun, says after much contemplation "I wonder if he has the same mind as the caterpillar"...and a few moments later, still studying the young butterfly, "but he doesn't have a Mom!"...

> Del Mar 1988
>
> In a meditative moment I watched the lacey shadow of a tree dancing on the gravel in a garden. I heard the gentle clicking-closed of a gate touched by the wind. An acorn dropped from a tree upon the ground...

Inner Life

David Nyberg on noticing:

> ...to examine and to become more precisely aware of what we do in fact notice in different contexts is to reintroduce ourselves to our active valuations...a way to discover what is new and what is habitual in our behavior...
>
> —(Nyberg 1971, 37)

As the days, months and years pass, the journalist lives with a keener sense of inner history and a perception of the texture and color of his life. Perusing old pages, one examines both the past and present, discovering patterns, themes and counter themes, motivic development, excursions to new "keys." Just as in music the underlying principles of repetition and change, unity and variety, will be discerned.

The past will be reflected in the changing mirror of your current self—smoothing out distortions and clarifying pictures. The nature of the reflecting surface always affects the quality of the image. Today's maturity and tomorrows' will provide new perspectives on who you are and what you are about. A lake in repose will clearly mirror the evergreens along the shore and on a morning of extreme serenity even capture the details of fleeting clouds while a rough-churned bay will fragment and disguise reflections.

Nearer to the truth, a pane of glass will reflect a scene even as it allows some transparency, creating a suggestive collage of seen and seen-through. The moment is distinctly viewed against a background of the formative past—closest perhaps to the complexity of experience.

You are the Tapestry

To use my favorite simile for the journal, it is like a loom upon which multicolored threads of experience weave themselves into a rich tapestry that is you. As the slim and widening shades of your ideas and attitudes, feelings, concerns, values, perceptions, pleasures and tastes accumulate and evolve, the journal becomes an art form in itself; your life, responding to and intertwining with the designs you weave, becomes more a work of art. The variegated strands will gather and grow in a most natural way.

I like especially the metaphor of a woven fabric for its two elements of warp and weft. It seems to me that the basic crosswise threads of the weft represent those parts of the self that are abiding, familiar, relatively unchanging—perhaps the "dyed-in-the-wool" hues—against which the daily choices are played out. I say relatively unchanging because I believe deeply in the ability of people to reshape themselves, exemplified by the message of this book itself. But these are gradual changes slowly tinted by the warp of experience—those new lengthwise threads that twine and twist into our lives and vary our being.

Ladera 1970

> I was informed once again this evening of the power music has to alter my spirit completely. I awoke from dozing to the positive radiance of Brahms' *Sextet for Strings* in B flat. I knew again and in a most exalted sense that music has a significant place, a pivotal place, in my life and I cannot deny it. It has at other times also stunned me into moments of the purest enlightenment and intuitive perception of the balance of things in my life and renewed my desire to search on, to live on with the simple knowledge that beautiful music exists and will be there for me again and again.

Del Mar 1977

> I feel closer to the truth of music, of each piece I play, or fragment I illustrate for a student, as I get closer to the truth of my own life.

Bits of Life to Save and Savor

We need not write everyday or feel compelled to record everything. Merely jot down bits of life that have meaning to you, that you want to save and savor— perhaps a dream that is striking, a quote from a book or article, a line of poetry, an important conversation, a memorable encounter or experience, an observation made on vacation, musings, reflections, reveries, hopes, memories, plans, even imaginary dialogues with people close to you or facets of yourself in search of understanding.

Larkspur 1974

...periwinkle leaps from the rich green bank over the narrow, leafy gully beside the street in Larkspur to grow in cracks of asphalt—like seeds of love, messages of hope leap over the spaces between people to grow and bloom in other hearts...

...plants clinging tenaciously in inhospitable cracks between the rocks of a retaining wall—alyssum, sedum, poppies—like ideas of determination and resolve...

Carmel 1974

I knew when I played the piano for Marianna and Bill that music was my true language, my authentic voice—that through it I had communicated to them more of me and what I had been experiencing of late than I had been able thus far in our visit to share through words.

Del Mar 1976

Kirsch on Adrienne Monnier (Los Angeles Times)[1]
...the grace, elegance, discretion of her style...La Maison des Amis des Livre, 1915-Rue de l'Odeon...inspired Sylvia Beach to found Shakespeare & Co...Monnier: "One can carry on no matter what business, no matter what profession, with a satisfaction that at certain moments has a real lyricism"...on books: "have loved them with rapture and have believed in the infinite power of the most beautiful"...a kind of nun of literature...

Imaginary Dialogues

I was introduced to the dialogue technique in 1977 during a remarkable weekend seminar at UCSD with a proponent of the Ira Progoff Journal process, Frances K. Heussenstamm. For our purposes, a conversation between you and your instrument, or even with music itself, where you delve into the source of any current conflict, might be revealing at this juncture. I found the imagined dialogue very helpful in dredging up buried emotions and understanding myself better.

The process is similar to dream interpretation, where one considers that each character in the dream story represents a facet of one's own personality.

Since you are writing the script, assuming each voice in turn, the thoughts you attribute to your imaginary conversant become very significant. His words issue

---

[1] From *Los Angeles Times* book review by Robert Kirsch (1976), of *The Very Rich Hours of Adrienne Monnier* by Richard McDougall.

from your mind and constitute *your perception* of him as well as your perception of how he sees you. Indeed, both voices are parts of you. The scripting of a fictional dialogue helps your feelings and thoughts unravel with surprising ease.

This process proves to be a creative way for you to help yourself—to go to root causes and uncover deep-seated attitudes.

You might have periodic conversations on paper as your thoughts evolve, perhaps with a former teacher, or an audience or a parent or sibling, as you feel inclined. This may help you articulate elusive feelings on subjects so close to your heart that it is sometimes difficult to sort them out. Later we will develop in more detail the idea of dialoguing particularly with that critical voice inside your head that sometimes causes mischief.

A Portrait in Words

As we will discover with dance, the journal has an integrating effect on its keeper. It becomes a representation, a synthesis of you as expressed through your choices, similar to an art collection that bears the aesthetic imprint of the collector—a portrait in words of your life process.

One begins to know oneself better and enjoy existence more—finding greater profundity and resonance in the world outside as one plumbs more deeply within.

Personal History

One fruitful subject for your journal, especially as you now embark upon this voyage toward more ease in performance, is your own personal musical history. You might first travel back and revisit your earliest musical memories, describing both events and your feelings about them as you now remember them. Throughout several sessions you could continue to record ensuing responses to musical happenings as you grew and evolved through childhood, adolescence, adulthood, until today. Again, this travelogue need not contain everything, but the highlights you select will be significant for their very memorability.

Some typical examples might include a memoir of a childhood teacher, a description of a particular recital experience, a vignette of a musical friend who was influential in your development, a piece of music you were touched by or struggled over, how you felt walking home from your clarinet lesson or while you listened to a concert artist rehearse the afternoon of his concert in your high school auditorium...how you felt when your parents asked you to play for visiting relatives after dinner or while you listened to the opera on the radio on Saturday afternoon...when you sang in the choir or played in the school band or listened to your older sister practice her violin in the morning. Whatever musical memory floats up to the surface is important to you.

The idea of perceiving one's story in terms of "stepping-stones" was another stimulating suggestion at the Progoff journal workshop. The process of scanning memories for significant turning points—whether a person, event, insight or reckoning—provided a fine structure for thinking through one's history. One could later dialogue with any of these memories.

It might be helpful, as well as pleasurable, to log your evolution as you proceed to try some of the approaches in this book. You will be more aware of the whole process if you attempt to express it in words. This will not be felt as an onerous task if you plan only to jot down an occasional insight or special moment of import to you. Sometimes the intent to make a brief jotting will take you easily to your pen and page where, once stimulated, you may find yourself digging more deeply into a thought and discovering more of your inner workings than you expected.

It may happen that you will want to do some sorting out, some rethinking, some pruning. Your journal will provide a good place for a contemplative sifting of new possibilities, new directions, new ideas that emerge on this adventure in learning.

You may begin to reformulate your attitude toward performance—how you study, what you expect from yourself, what you want to give, how you relate to your instrument, why and how you feel about music.

Be open to change. Welcome it. Change can come from examining feelings, trying to understand them and choosing how you prefer to feel—resetting your own course. You are the captain and you control this voyage into self-discovery and improvement.

An artist grows by asking questions.

As the pianist Josef Hofmann said, not "the worship of names, the unquestioning acquiescence in traditional conceptions" but "rather a close examination of every popular notion, a severe testing of every tradition by the touchstone of self-thinking...will help an artist to find himself and to see, what he does see, with his own eyes" (Hofmann 1976, 17).

Looking into the Past

Looking into the past for current enlightenment can be useful. A natural image I encountered one day while out walking brought this concept home to me. Later we will develop more fully the idea of symbolizing from nature, but this particular image may spark your thinking at this point. I entered it in my journal.

Del Mar 1983

> Walking today on a hillside street, I noticed some new, lustrous, yellow-green growth sprouting from the mature branches of a bush. My glance shifted down to the deep natural mulch on the ground at the base of the bush—a melange of dried leaves and berries, bits of dead twig, fallen blossoms that never opened, faded petals, all now ripened into a nourishing organic matter that was providing food for the bush, making new growth possible—like the debris of the past in all of us, composed of memories, experiences, mistakes as well as successes, hopes, disappointments, joys. I thought: out of this emotional debris comes the material for future growth. We can't exist without it. We can grow when we learn from it. One becomes a new person derived from it and because of it. Don't rake the past away. Make a nourishing "compost" out of it and use it. Let it help you.

Your past musical experiences will provide the seeds for understanding your current feelings. Bring them out into the light, record them, reflect upon them. Don't be afraid of them. They are part of you and need to be recognized, analyzed and dealt with. If you rake them neatly away, you may be denying yourself some significant discoveries and the potential for fresh new growth.

What Art Does For Us

It might be helpful to plumb another level in our consideration of the artistic experience before we go on to develop the nature symbols.

I read a poem recently which affected me powerfully and led me to contemplate what art does for us. Perhaps it will be a touchstone for our discussion. I believe it to be a fine example of how art works as well as a rare cameo of human expression.

DAVID
(Nov. 4-8, 1971)

> When you came down that slow canal
> into light,
> you thought it was the wrong country—
> France, maybe, the Seine—
> and never even waved to us,
> but kept on going till you disappeared
> under a far bridge.

> What difficulty we had then
> with language, saying *chromosomes*
> and holding the word close like a replica
> of you, or the brief glimpse
> you'd given us: brown hair,
> mouth curved in the trajectory
> of a summer star.
>
> What could we do but roam the narrow streets,
> as if the light rain
> falling and falling around our eyes
> would let us remember you
> in the way the mist
> never quite lifted
> from rooftops and spires.
>
> Little prince, when I sit in the park these days
> on my lunch hour, dark birds
> swarm at my feet. I open a paper bag and break
> bread in your name.
>
> —(Dorian Brooks Kottler 1988, 49)

Before you go on, reread the poem a few times and think about the experience. How did you feel as you read the poem? What did it give to you and how did it accomplish this? What happens during an artistic event? What does art do for people? What is an artist? When are we expressing creative or artistic impulses in our lives? In your life?

In this poem and all fine art, I believe the artist transmutes experience into a work of beauty, communicating to the receiver the emotions evoked by the experience. The content represented by a symbolic language is not always so concrete an event as it is in this poem—sometimes only a mood or a vision or, in music, the most abstract of the arts, a series of essences shaped in sound and time. The poet's transformation of profound loss in this case would not only be a comfort to a reader who has known the same loss but it increases the ability of any reader to empathize.

In reaching out to understand the offering, finding the sensitivity within to feel *with* the artist, the receiver grows. The poet has mined her soul to find the nugget of truth and forge it into art. The reader's comprehension is expanded by this knowledge of another human's experience. Our appreciation of life is enhanced by a generous gift—the metamorphosis of pain into beauty.

Thus art is a meeting—of creator and receiver, human being and human being, one reaching out to the fullest extent of his ability to render experience in symbolic form and share it; the other reaching out as far as possible to understand and receive. He apprehends the message to the extent to which he appreciates and feels the words and thoughts and imagery of the poet, finding resonance within himself—the commonality, the ability to comprehend and share.

Thus art is expanding; art is sensitizing. It is comforting. It restores and sends courage from person to person. It performs a necessary healing function for us and it inspires as well. One is touched by the beauty and transformed even as the artist is affected by experience and transmutes it into beauty, perhaps even needs to transmute it in order to digest it.

The poet's well-hewn metaphor opens for us a door to her vision of experience. In this way, fantasy helps us deal with reality. Meeting on the threshold of art, we help each other, communicate with each other, understand life together, know our humanness.

Perhaps this perspective will give us a more universal view of our experience as communicators of great art, helping us to go beyond, to travel outside ourselves, to prize our role in human sharing.

The Power of Music

The writings of Oliver Sacks, neurologist and poet in the purest sense of the word, exemplify this issue on several levels. His book, *A Leg to Stand On* (Sacks 1984), especially illustrates the power of music to heal and restore, as song enables him to descend alone from a mountain peak with a severely painful leg injury and later, a recording of Mendelssohn's *Violin Concerto* rouses him to learn to walk again.

Toiling down the mountainside, exhausted and faint:

> There came to my aid now melody, rhythm and music (what Kant calls the "quickening" art). Before crossing the stream, I had *muscled* myself along...Now, so to speak, I was *musicked* along...I fell into a rhythm...Now, I no longer had to think about going too fast or too slow. I got into the music, got into the swing, and this ensured that my *tempo* was right. I found myself perfectly coordinated by the rhythm...the musical beat was generated within me, and all my muscles responded obediently—all save those in my left leg which seemed silent—or mute? Does not Nietzsche say that when listening to music, we "listen with our muscles?"

> Somehow, with this "music," it felt much less like a grim anxious struggle. There was even a certain primitive exuberance, such as Pavlov called "muscular gladness."

> I had no room for...fear...because I was filled to the brim with music...the music of my muscle-orchestra playing—"the silent music of the body," in Harvey's lovely phrase. With this playing, the musicality of my motion, I myself became the music...
>
> —(pp. 30, 31)

And later, in the hospital, when struggling to walk again:

> And suddenly—into the silence, the silent twittering of motionless frozen images—came music, glorious music, Mendelssohn, *fortissimo*! Joy, life, intoxicating movement! And, as suddenly, without thinking, without intending whatever, I found myself walking, easily-joyfully, *with* the music...
>
> ...*I remembered how to walk*. All of a sudden I remembered walking's natural, unconscious rhythm and melody...it came hand-in-hand with the Mendelssohn rhythm and tune. There was an abrupt and absolute leap...from the awkward, artificial, mechanical walking...to an unconscious, natural-graceful, musical movement.
>
> —(pp. 144, 145)

I often recommend this book to music teachers and performers to rekindle a sense of wonder at the uncanny might of our medium, a flame we must keep lit. It is a potent antidote to doubt or burn-out or bogging down in routine. Just as the symbolic idiom of music reached out to Sacks in time of need, his telling of the story through the art of language resounds in our hearts, stirring us with devotion to our work and summoning up renewed courage to embrace life fully.

Reason and Fantasy

Further food for thought on the subject of the relation of imagination/fantasy to reason/reality comes from the Polish writer Witold Gombrowicz. Although I question his suggestion that poets feel a "helplessness in the face of reality"—a canard that the David poem nicely refutes—another statement makes a cogent point:

> ... the imperialism of reason is horrible. Whenever reason notices that some part of reality eludes it, it immediately lunges at it to devour it.
>
> —(Gombrowicz 1988)

This omnivorous nature of reason is something for us to ruminate upon. As civilized adults we learn to respect the hard light of reason but as musicians and performers we also need to inhabit the realm of imagination, to find the artist within each of us and make contact more frequently and fully with that artistic self, to develop the artistic impulse, to cultivate the ability to pretend, to fantasize, to capture and recreate moods, to render the subjective—all intrinsic to our ability to interpret and, an ultimate requirement of performance, to let go.

Obviously, the voice of reason, or the critical faculty, as we shall see, has an essential role in laying out the whole process of study in preparation for performance. We need to organize our work, to schedule, to plan sensibly, to deal with the myriad practical details of our lives, to heed our ears and sensibilities, to evaluate and alter, to cultivate refinement in our interpretation. *We need to assimilate the voice of the critic into our process,* to give our "evaluator" a constructive role—partly because we vitally need its analytic strength but also to prevent it from becoming a destructive voice during preparation or performance. It is constantly needed throughout our preparation but in performance the letting go is an indispensable partner, even a dominant one.

Symbolizing and Fluidity

Carmel 1984

...I saw a tree leaning out from a bank beside the path...an "L-shaped" tree, *which had begun its life horizontally* because of early obstacles and conditions. It had finally reached a clear space where it was able to right itself and begin to reach straight up to the sky—erect and tall and vertical at last!...the transformative effects of environment!

Del Mar 1985

Today at the end of a long hike, climbing a steep street quite close to home, I noticed a little rivulet of water streaming down the hill right alongside the curb. It was a quiet sunny day...the air was still, so I was able to hear a faint, bubbling, musical sound singing from the humble little brook and I noticed that it came from those areas where stones and pebbles had lodged and the little stream had to gurgle its way over the stones. It made its lovely music at those very places where it had to overcome obstacles!!

Del Mar 1985

Synchronicity!--today received in mail booklet from Jungian Institute on new series of seminars...discovered in longer quote from book of poetry by Wendell Berry: "The mind that is not baffled is not employed. The impeded stream is the one that sings"...the same bit of nature-wisdom offered to me by my little brook!

From our previous discussion of art and the symbolic treatment of experience, it becomes clear that "making connections" is a prime ingredient in the artistic process. The composer translates his world into sound-symbols, the visual artist expresses his with shape, line and color, the writer, words, and the dancer, forms in space.

Activities that stimulate a performer to know a *fluidity* between realms of experience, exercising this capacity to make connections, will ease his entry into the composer's realm of meaning. And so, in addition to the journal, our exploration of a richer life within brings us to the notion of symbolizing from nature—finding enlightening parallels between the beauty of natural phenomena and the dynamics of our own lives.

The patterns of nature, when we learn to attend them, offer a simple wisdom in their beauty, clarity and balance—a wisdom which is clearly ours to begin with, but which is touched and crystallized in a moment of recognition when we are in contact with our deepest inner resources. Cultivating a receptivity to the nourishing presence of nature will allow us to make such creative leaps.

When I look at a stand of trees or a wave or a bush and it suddenly seems to be making a statement—a direct, unadorned statement about life, there is harmony in that moment. The bush unifies one's vision, bringing together the aesthetic, psychological, cognitive and imaginative faculties with all of one's life experiences.

In an essay on education, the philosopher Martin Buber poetically described this very aspect of human potential:

> Human inwardness is in origin a polyphony in which no voice can be 'reduced' to another, in which the unity cannot be grasped analytically, but only heard in the present harmony.
>
> —(Buber [1947] 1955, 86)

Much has been said of right brain and left brain distinctions and the horizon keeps shifting on that particular territory. But I think we can fairly safely say that we recognize states of mind in ourselves that can be identified as more or less cognitive or imaginative. I also hold that a full and rich interplay between the two is usually coursing in the presence of great art or great science.

Indeed, Howard Gardner, eminent psychologist with Harvard's Project Zero which has been investigating this very realm for twenty years, says "we are becoming increasingly convinced of the importance of metaphoric processes in the life of the individual" and that "we also encounter metaphor in the highest reaches of creativity, where someone is articulating a scientific theory or describing a subtle mood" (Gardner 1982, 166).

Also germane to our discussion is Gardner's selection from Aristotle, offering that the Greek philosopher "considered metaphor a sign of genius, believing that the individual who could make unusual connections was a person of special gifts." Gardner goes on to define metaphor as "the capacity to perceive a resemblance between elements from two separate domains or areas of experience and to link them together in linguistic form." This is precisely what we do in symbolizing from nature (Gardner 1982, 161).

I believe that all human beings have these "special gifts", that the capacity to make "unusual connections" can be developed (or refound) and that cultivating it will enhance our skills as performing artists. This ability, which I have referred to as fluidity between realms of experience, was present in vast quantity in early childhood, when each of us exhibited a natural creative aptitude and flair that I'm sure your parents will be happy to corroborate. In those days, we took crayon or pen to paper with unselfconscious delight to express in pictorial or verbal symbols (or both) our deepest urges as well as our passing fancies. We sang and danced and made theater out of the most modest ingredients. We produced endless variations on our favorite themes every day of our young lives, deriving pleasure and fulfillment from this creative play.

> In his *Critique of Pure Reason* Immanuel Kant cited two miracles as standing out above all others: the starry heaven above and the moral law we all carry within ourselves. I would dare to propose a third which has long struck me as equally marvelous: the creative activity of the young child.
>
> —(Gardner 1982, 83)

There is no agreement among scholars as to what happens to this fount of energy and freedom approximately when children enter school but I strongly feel that if it was there once, within each of us, we can reconnoiter and rediscover it. Indeed, whenever you write a letter, have a meaningful conversation with a friend, design a table or a quilt, devise a new recipe or a garden plan, you are exercising your creative impulse, your ability to imagine and transform the substance of your imagining into reality.

By tapping into this source, we can bring that youthful delight in creating together with our adult insights to discover rich layers of meaning in our lives.

We need to recognize that we're talking about cultivating openness and sensitivity in general, qualities which are often repressed by adults in our culture. Artists value these traits and grow through them. We musicians need them—we teachers too.

You have the capacity to made connections within you. I think you will enjoy employing it to learn how the truths of nature can find a resonance in matters of your own mind.

An Image Completed

Del Mar 1974
...the new capacity, full blown now, to perceive images of nature as symbols of life's meaning...they leap through vision into my consciousness and coalesce there the fragments, the threads of thought awaiting shape, bringing me moments of rare illumination...

I have always found comfort in nature, although I noticed a remarkable intensification of my sensitivity to the metaphoric life of natural things about fifteen years ago. I begin by sharing with you an image that has been with me much of my life. It came to me spontaneously when I was fairly young, helping me through difficult moments in life and recently completing, fulfilling itself in a very interesting way.

One day, many years back, I noticed how particularly beautiful are the *very tops* of trees: how richly green they are, the extraordinary, inexorable way they reach straight up to the sun. They grow tall, simply, directly, undeterred by obstacles, healthy, strong. They keep growing, *keep reaching* with an inevitability I admired. I found those treetops most renewing of my energy. I remember in adolescent times of stress and even later in life gaining much strength from seeing and thinking about those top-most branches, feeling a sustaining support, even an inner glow from a wish to emulate them, to grow as tall within, to reach as bravely for the warmth of the sun in the infinite sky.

And then, a couple of years ago, while out on one of my regular walks, a stately old tree caught my attention—its powerful trunk led my eye from those treetops down to the green earth and into the earth. I imagined the huge network of roots reaching deep down into the dark soil for nourishment and spreading broadly for security. "Of course!" It struck me in a flash: one needs to be deeply and securely rooted in order to grow with vigor, to be centered in one's work, one's values, one's principles, one's culture, one's friendships, one's family—gaining nourishment from these deep, substantial roots.

The image was complete now through my awareness of the tree's connection with the *source* of its strength. The finishing of this circle of knowledge through the image of the tree was very satisfying for me. How right that the youthful symbol which was so appropriate and helpful in those early years would lead me organically to its source and my own source of sustenance, comfort, enlightenment in my mature years.

I have found it exciting to learn that philosopher Susan Langer in her 1941 work *Philosophy in a New Key,* "posited a basic and pervasive human need to symbolize, to invent meanings, and to invest meanings in one's world. It was a property of the human mind to search for and find significance everywhere, to transform experience constantly to uncover new meanings" [Gardner 1982, 50).

I believe this to be true; furthermore, I believe that this human capacity might be developed and lead to heightened personal and artistic fulfillment.

Beethoven, Einstein, Casals all walked often in the country or by the sea for contact with the essential truths of nature, for insights into life, art, science. They would go to nature to seek out the wisdom it houses but the wisdom was already deep within them. It can be touched and brought to the surface, to our conscious awareness, by the symbols of nature. We can observe these images and be altered by them if we are open to the possibility of noticing them, sensitized to their symbolic messages. The trees and bushes and streams and clouds and wild flowers seem to suggest answers to questions we unconsciously pose, questions we want or need to ask.

How It Works

How does it work? The analogy we make is an imagistic link, a creative leap between the tree and our own inner search.

We look at the tree, admire its beauty, feel its comforting simplicity and companionship, notice its modest existence, how it gives us its beauty so easily, undemandingly, unexpectantly, (as we will give to our audiences). We appreciate the gift; it is disarming; we feel open and safe. We sense our affinity with its liveness. We see the way it lives, the way we live and in the light of that intimate exchange of beauty and shared life, we are enabled to realize a truth the tree represents by its very existence. It appears to exemplify with proverbial power a verity that casts light on a situation or problem in our own life. Thus the tree seems to speak to us, offering a suggestion, a reality uncannily intrinsic to our own thought processes and germane to whatever it is we are grappling with at the moment.

In this moment of inspiration, or epiphany, we make contact with our source of creativity. The flash, the new connection flows from ready access among realms of awareness—imagination, intellect, personality, aesthetic, intuition.

There is something about the truth of natural things that makes us, helps us, confront our own truth. The tree exists in balance, responding to its environment honestly, with a will to survive and without any pretense or digression. Perhaps it is that balance also to which we respond. The tree lives as best it can with the conditions of its surroundings and grows to be as healthy and beautiful as it is able.

People who live high up above the Pacific ocean on the cliffs of Big Sur say the daily sight of that vast majestic sea stretching endlessly and broadly to the sky compels them to confront themselves honestly, something an artist must do.

And how powerfully Prince Andrew's perspective was altered in Tolstoy's *War and Peace* by the sight of "the lofty sky" as he lay on the earth after being struck down in battle.

> He opened his eyes...but he saw nothing. Above him there was now nothing but the sky—the lofty sky, not clear but still immeasurably lofty, with grey clouds gliding slowly across it. "How quiet, peaceful, and solemn, not at all...as we ran, shouting and fighting...how differently do those clouds glide across that lofty infinite sky! How was it I did not see that lofty sky before? And how happy I am to have found it at last! Yes! All is vanity, all falsehood, except that infinite sky. There is nothing, nothing but that."
> —(Oxford University Press edition p. 396)

Nature—the sky, the ocean, a stand of trees, a weed—all help us to find our native sense, our own most natural path. We all share life—the supreme gift.

It is an artistic act to make the leap. If the end is deeper self-understanding, it is also a meditative, contemplative act—an act of self-examination facilitated by the tree. This is, after all, what art does. It strikes a resonance with the receiver's experience causing that sense of self-discovery, that "yes—how true" feeling.

Again, we see a creative act as a new connection. In this sense, there are no new ideas—only new connections.

In order to take that deep plunge into the music vital to our concentration as performers, we must connect personally with the music as art, at this deep level of self-realization. We need to be open to this interactive process as we interpret a chosen work. In a profound study of music there is the exciting potential not only for self-discovery and change, but for an organic bonding with the very metabolism of the music. *We need this penetration to the marrow and we need to stay there during performance.*

Aesthetic Order

The more we delve into the symbolizing process to understand it fully, the more it resembles the process of art appreciation. It involves a sensitization to visual elements and to the principles of their relating, both of which are also active in responding to any art form with a visual component. Let us imagine ourselves out for a walk to feel how this might be true for each of us.

You are walking briskly along a path in one of your favorite places. You hear bird song, you feel the warm sun sifting through tree branches and dabbing at your cheek. The air is fresh and bracing, especially after some hours of indoor work. You feel your muscles warming up, loosening, and your thoughts unwinding a bit—with threads of new ideas weaving in occasionally, memories fleeting by, immediate sensations pouring into your pool of awareness and mingling there with old images, feelings, perceptions, attitudes.

In this fluid state of mind, relaxed and perceptive, your attention is captured by a large old live oak tree, darkly silhouetted against the sky. You notice its graceful swirling branches that seem to dance with one another in patterns that move together and apart—sometimes curving in parallel sweeps, at times bowing, bending toward or away from each other slightly—and then you suddenly see: "yes! like the lives of people."

Somehow this is a reassuring thought. You realize you have been musing about friendship and the dance of the branches make the waxing and waning of proximity quite natural and acceptable, an organic part of the total picture of life. The beautiful and well-balanced overall design of the tree helps you to see the movement of peoples' lives as part of a larger pattern.

The tree offers illumination as well as beauty. It helps you to find your own intuitive wisdom and puts you in touch with the same life energy that sustains and nourishes it. The tree has become a sign of your path, your inner truth. If the thought comes to you, it has meaning for you.

To return to our analogy with art, you responded to the curving lines formed by the branches. Your eye was then led along the pathways of those lines from one to another and you enjoyed the various ways they related to each other, the patterns they revealed. You began to apprehend the larger composition, the structure of the whole—how the diversity of the branches was intrinsic to the beauty of the tree. Perhaps the perception of aesthetic order, of repetition with variety, balance with asymmetry, helped you make the leap to the same organizing elements, the same sense of "rightness" and rhythm in life.

Movement and Change in Art and Life

The mention of rhythm in the movement of the branches as well as in the patterns of friends' relating suggests a most important aspect of art and life that may explain, in part, how it is that art holds such meaning for human beings. I speak of movement and change.

In any art form movement is vital. Stasis is death to art; change is its very essence. "That is a boring book," Johnny says, "not enough action." And a sophisticated reviewer might make a similar comment about a new play. It is clear that the same is true for each of us. We need change, movement, variety. We need to get away sometimes; we also need to return to the familiar, comforting nest—hopefully refreshed, changed by the mobility and novel experience.

Later in Chapter IV we will discuss principles of composition which are deeply integrative, hidden elements in the pieces we study, including the idea of unity and variety recently mentioned. But surrounding any such structural ideals is the all-encompassing notion of movement and its corollary, change. We find it in art and in nature; we need it in our lives. An ordering physical principle is at work as the branches grow and form their pattern. In a sense, we discover the underlying, organizational principle when we glean the message. The tree's shape, and yours, is a result of its genetic endowment and its response to environment. At the bottom, this is the basis that makes comparisons appropriate.

Being "Moved"

The poet Denise Levertov discerns a fresh connection between the concept of movement and another well-worn usage of the word. As poets can be, she is sensitive to words and illumines our thinking with a new look at an old word.

In her book, *The Poet in the World*, referring to the familiar notion of being "moved" by art, she offers that the work of art indeed "sets in motion forces within" us, suggesting that something actually moves within, is reordered and changed in that powerful moment; the mental and emotional furniture is rearranged and we are altered (Levertov 1973, 98).

So art does this for us too; it stimulates, it is generative. It gets things moving inside us, "forces" already there that await a catalyst. I find in my journal, after the Levertov quote, a note with a flavor of revelation: "This is what happened with Sally's paintings that evening when I felt so 'moved'"! I remember well how a poem was born of my friend's paintings. I don't write poems very often, but occasionally I will have an experience that, it seems, can only be expressed and somehow must be expressed through poetry.

I had thoroughly enjoyed a lovely series of mussel paintings Sally displayed that evening, one after another, in the warm atmosphere she and her husband had created in their cottage. She had greatly enlarged the shells to explore all the subtle variants of hue and design on their inner surfaces. For three days afterward I could hardly do anything else but write my poem.

SALLY'S PAINTINGS, SEEN ON A SABBATH EVE

a mussel
the soft inside
of a mussel shell
open
offering me
the gift
of itself

inner surface
curving
smooth
like Alice
grown
to nearly fill
the canvas

giant shell
my equal
bare
you look at me
share
your life and
color

flowing
creamy white
through lavender
to ever deeper
shades
not quite
to purple

more mussels
many
every rendering
a journey
through new spaces
some blues
soft rubs of green
shapes that dream
within the larger forms
melting
shifting
singing

they *did* sing to me
I can hear them now
and know that fusion of *all* forms
seen
heard
touched
ultimate art
can it be defined?
it is a glowing place when you know it
a spacious stretching of the mind
to soul and back
the body fused with light
resounding with song
it is like love

A Subtle Process

As we will discover later with dance movement, we cannot force this process of symbolizing. We cannot will it; we can only welcome it—unselfconsciously permitting it to happen. In dance and music performance we will absorb the music until we feel it deeply within. The same is true here. Look around and relish the sights and sounds and sensations of nature. Let yourself absorb—feel, hear, see, smell, sense. The connections will happen in your mind when you are ready and the moment is right. Enjoying, noticing, feeling open and alert, a thought will be born.

This is a subtle process. The act of pinning it down in order to describe it and direct another seems to do violence to it. It is like a luminous bubble that pops into nothingness when you try to take it in your hand.

Exercise seems to encourage the flow of creative juices but don't be disappointed if it doesn't happen immediately. I don't have a significant insight every time I go out walking. But I always feel refreshed after a walk. My thoughts often sort themselves out and I return home with some new resolve or plan.

Walking with Nature

The renewal of energy is always there for you even when the philosophic moments of inspiration are not. The idea of walking in beautiful natural places is, in itself, something I enthusiastically recommend—daily if possible, but as often as you can and long enough to clear your mind, stimulate your circulation, feel like you've used your muscles and most important, refresh your spirit. Perhaps we are also learning at an unconscious level when we feel this renewal.

An hour is great but even twenty minutes or a half hour will be very helpful. I should warn you, this makes you feel so good that it tends to become addictive—surely one of the healthiest habits you'll ever acquire.

Earth

There is an energy to be found in nature, a life force to be felt—a permanence that echoes in us because we are of the earth. We come from the earth and we return to the earth. We share the same basic elements—hydrogen, oxygen and carbon compounds with the rocks, trees, birds. We're made of the same fundamental material. Perhaps we need contact with our simpler beginnings to feel complete. Modern life instead usually sequesters us in our minds, in our houses, in our cars, surrounded by all the artificial albeit necessary or rewarding creations of civilization.

As modern living has taken us away from nature, people seem to feel a pull back to it—the Sunday picnic in the park, the drive into the country, the beloved visit to a cousin's farm, that needed weekend in the mountains or at the ocean.

On a smaller scale, you can satisfy this deep human need more often. If you live near mountains, ocean, canyon, meadow or country roads, go to them. But one can also find much beauty, natural shapes and creatures in a nearby park or even in a neighborhood walk—birds, trees, bushes, flowers, hills, clouds, horizons are all around you when you tune in to them.

If you walk often, you will begin to revel in the sense of renewal inherent in the seasonal cycles—birth, growth, waning, rebirth like the return of a melody in a fresh new key. You will find variations on a theme in the multitude of versions of the daisy as you become closer to the earth.

If you walk to the grocery story or post office or library, you will enjoy using your own legs rather than a fuel-eating machine for a functional purpose—to get you to a place you need for health and sustenance. There is a special satisfaction in using our own human energy to move about in space and get things we need. Our ancestors engaged in this activity daily, when there was a natural, intimate association with the earth, for nurture, survival, religion.

CHAPTER IV

BEDROCK KNOWLEDGE—OUR COGNITIVE PREPARATION

WHAT-TO-DO

Intimate Knowledge of Structure and Specifics

We have already acknowledged the fundamental importance for confident performance of knowing the music in intimate detail and *knowing* that you know it beyond a doubt. Now we describe a system of study which solidly plants this information in mind and ears and fingers—both the structure of a piece and its specifics—at the same time building the foundation for a psychological support system throughout the piece with ready recall of structural units, their relationships and starting points.

One Performs the Way One Practices

As we enter this analytic phase, a word of caution is appropriate. Through first hand experience I have learned that *one performs the way one practices*. For example, if you unduly emphasize the intellectual over the emotional this will be reflected in a rather dry cerebral performance. If your approach is overwhelmingly physical, without sufficient thought given to form, mood, or musical facts, the possibility of an accurate but less meaningful rendition is likely, and that accuracy will be prey to memory lapses. Of course, if "feeling" alone is exercised (along with a solely intuitive reveling in sound) at the expense of analysis or technique, the results can be both disorderly and amorphous. The ideal is a process which integrates all the elements at each stage of study.

Integration of All Elements at Each Stage of Study; Conscious and Unconscious

Alvin Toffler so aptly said, in his foreword to physicist Ilya Prigogine's enlightening book *Order Out of Chaos*:

> One of the most highly developed skills in contemporary Western civilization is dissection: the split-up of problems into their smallest possible components. We are good at it. So good, we often forget to put the pieces back together again.
> —(Toffler 1984, xi)

We do recognize in music study the value of dissection. Indeed, we have all observed in practice the efficiency and ease of learning small bits of information through isolation and repetition. But what is the process of reintegration and how does it function?

In an effective plan of study both conscious and unconscious forces are at work putting the pieces back together again. At the conscious level, even as we break down and study a phrase intervallically, rhythmically, harmonically, texturally, we can be aware that the bits together express an *idea* that we hear, feel and know. The composer's argument progresses not in a note-by-note sequence but by *musical ideas* and our task is to decipher the notational code and determine the essential spirit, the particular sound of each idea, working at how best to project this "musical meaning" through the sculpting of dynamics, details of articulation and texture, variation in touch, shading, balance, etc.—that is, the process of interpretation, the realization of the text in sound. We seek a beautiful correlation between each musical idea and a *kind* of sound.

Then we examine the relationship of one idea to the next, and that to the following, until we rebuild the entire work and perceive its overall architecture, noting structural high points, emotional peaks and valleys. As we reconstruct the work, we might also consider larger integrating features such as harmonic schemes, forms (both generalized and particular), unifying compositional techniques, thematic metamorphosis and development, and artistic principles such as economy of means, unity and variety, contrast and stylistic consistency.

What is acting at the unconscious level to put the pieces back together is the remarkable oneness of our human sensory mechanism including "heart," mind and neuromuscular system. As we play our instrument, the body works as a synchronous whole. A constant feedback apparatus is at work, completing a simultaneous cycle of feeling, producing, hearing, evaluating and altering our sound.

Physical and intellectual learning are meshed together in the repetition of a phrase as we work to develop the kinesthetic response. Artistic and emotional involvement are allied closely with the physical and intellectual and all are controlled by the brain, the ultimate unifying organ. Indeed while engaged in music making, the ability of a human being to synthesize diverse elements with the energy of his own thrust is nothing short of remarkable.

We need to *allow* this fine responsive system to stay tuned to the essence of each idea at all times to receive the composer's message as it unfolds, sensitively in touch with the character even as we master the basic facts of each phrase, then each section, then the whole—never lapsing into a purely analytic or mechanical routine.

The performance bond is being forged during practice. If we are emotionally engaged, in constant relation with the content, in constant contact with this energy source from the composer, aware of how the parts of a work relate to each other and build into the whole and actively contributing our own unique personal energy, wholeness will be projected. Well-integrated in practice, it will be well-wrought in performance.

Thus, *how one practices is of utmost importance,* not only for the most efficient and effective learning method but for the model it plants in our nervous system which will be realized in performance. Every minute of practice is patterning the neurons for performance.

What is a Musical Idea?

Let us take a moment to consider exactly what constitutes an idea in musical terms. At the most basic level, one might say a musical idea is composed of sounds organized in aesthetically pleasing patterns which render them orderly and coherent.

Furthermore, the musical thought communicates a character, mood and energy which is perceived in emotional terms by the listener or participant and attributed with personal "meaning." This reception of the idea, which must be considered part of its definition, is elusive and rather mysterious—a function of the ineffable power of music to affect human beings deeply.

Through nonverbal, private associations which operate unconsciously—psychologically and imagistically—each of us is stirred uniquely by the evocative symbols of musical sound.

Our job is to discern the patterns, analyze them as musical events, sense the particular nature of the energy and project the meaning as we feel it. The result will be an interpretation inspired by a lively awareness of the physical realities of sound. The deeper one's understanding of the musical substance of ideas and construction, the more penetrating the interpretation.

This process can be broken down into several levels to understand it more accurately.

Levels of Analysis

Experiencing music is a whole act. However, understanding the component ideas well enough to project them persuasively and perform with confidence requires thoughtful exploration of their parts. Taking a structured approach to analysis with defined layers and categories will stimulate your observations, encourage precision in your comments and insure that you consider all the ways of thinking—neither omitting any nor substituting one for another.

The delineation of the levels is offered as an analytic background for the activities of study that follow.

The most fundamental task of analysis, having decided upon the borders of an idea, is to determine its musical *facts*—i.e., the actual details of melody, rhythm, etc. which together constitute the idea.

We then climb up to the next level of discerning the *patterns* that enliven these facts, that create the musical event. Thus we discover the musical syntax, the artfully conceived order which results in coherence—an arrangement of the parts as a comprehensible entity.

Next we try to sensitize ourselves to the *physical thrust* of these happenings, in an effort to describe the dynamic energy of the idea—the physics if you will. This is a colorful, exciting stage which will kindle your imagination. We ask ourselves how the phrase physically enters and affects the atmosphere of the room. What is its impact?

This feeling approach to the body and power of a musical idea flows quite naturally into the imagery of the next level (e.g., weighty becomes portentous); trying to keep them separate makes us more precise and aware of the words we use and exactly what they mean. Such discipline can lead to a sharper, clearer definition of the composer's ideas.

Moving up to this next level of description, we may develop a richer relatedness to the idea by finding words and images that epitomize its *intrinsic character* or personality. This is a highly personal area of analysis; because it is self-referential, the meaning attributed by each of us will be different. Such subjectivity creates a kind of danger zone, since no one can say for certain what a given musical idea is about (perhaps not even the composer). It is important to allow this process of personal association to occur, but it is just as important to preface such comments with "I feel" or "it sounds to me like..." in acknowledgement of the subjectivity.

Then we relate ideas to each other according to *function*, continuing on up to larger *structural areas* and to an appreciation of the *form* of the whole.

"Re-Composing"

To get as close as possible to knowing a piece as the composer might have intended, we use a process I call "re-composing." We want to build a solid foundation in detail. Of course the performer does not consciously and continually call forth these specifics during performance; he is operating on a higher integrative level of ideas, emotions, moods, momentum, relationships but he enjoys, as we shall see, a security that comes from the certainty of this unconscious bedrock knowledge of the music.

It should be stated emphatically that reliance on finger-memory alone is extremely hazardous. One needs certainly to build those kinesthetic patterns deeply into the muscles, but one needs also to have a thorough cognitive grasp of musical happenings. Without such awareness one is at sea during performance, totally dependent on the muscles—one's direction subject to any passing current.

Determine and Mark Articulation of Ideas

Our first task is to determine and mark in the score the beginning and end of each musical idea, simply by playing and listening for a sense of completion or partial completion. Subunits are helpful too. (See Example 1)

Example 1: Intermezzo in A Opus 118/2 by Johannes Brahms

Even this early, fairly primitive effort encourages sensitivity to phrasing as we listen for content, for punctuation, for sentences that develop a story line. Thus we are tuning in to the "inner curve" of the piece as opposed to surface features— sensing emotional content, intrinsic message, physical vitality, excitement and relaxation.

Music has been compared to language in many contexts. It is a useful analogy despite the subtle differences. We do hear phrases, sentences, paragraphs, even chapters, in most music and we can discern points of articulation or punctuation. All musicians will not agree on every demarcation point, but I think many will agree on most.

Sometimes the joinings are ambiguous or overlapping and the object is not to ascertain "the" ultimate and indisputable delineation. What is important is for the performer to hear and decide which divisions make sense to him, for these have the personal meaning that will last in the memory. It is equally important to be consistent in placing articulation points—for example, in similar or parallel passages whether to join a transitional idea to the previous or subsequent thought.

This initial task of determining and marking phrases is critical for three reasons.

1. It creates brief working units which our systems seem to digest most efficiently;
2. It gets us thinking structurally right at the outset;
3. Most important, it establishes immediately and clearly a foundation for our starting point support system in performance.

Study Musical Ideas and Their Realization

The next step is not merely to learn the notes in each phrase, but to *study the musical idea* and its realization as an artistic entity, in fine detail and from every perspective—melody, rhythm, meter, *tempo,* register and range, harmony, texture, touch, dynamics, pedaling, basic thrust or gesture, mood, "message," function, and on to fine shading, nuance and other subtle matters of timing and balance.

Punctuation and Enunciation

In so doing we may distinguish "outer phrasing" from "inner phrasing." The former refers to the division of the music into coherent ideas, the *punctuation* of the narrative in terms of thoughts to be communicated as expressive entities in themselves. The latter concerns what I call the *enunciation* of the effects within the phrase, matters such as slurs, rests, *staccatos,* accents, which require careful attention to project precisely and clearly, and which contribute to the apt delivery of the whole idea.

Examples of Elements to Analyze

What are the kinds of specifics we are analyzing? This is, of course, a subject as varied as music itself and expandable at great length but here we will only suggest a few ideas dealing with melody, rhythm, harmony, texture, thrust, and function. The examining of details and deliberating on how best to interpret them are highly rewarding and exciting activities, almost endless in possibility, the very heart of the musician's life. Many critical discoveries about the music are to be made at this fundamental level. A confident interpretation will be generated by and built upon these facts.

I remember the elation I felt when I discovered, in a passage of Brahms' *Intermezzo* Opus 118 No. 2 that seemed the most tender moment of the piece, an inversion of the main theme. It was like a wise and cherished friend saying in conversation, "but here's another way of looking at it." (Compare Examples 1 and 2.)

Example 2: Intermezzo in A Opus 118/2 by Johannes Brahms

On a revisit to another *Intermezzo*, the graceful rippling Opus 117 No. 2, I noticed that the full tonic chord is never heard in root position until the very last phrase of the piece—a fact which explains the gently hovering quality of the piece and makes that rich resonant B flat tonic so satisfying when it finally comes.

Melody

To take melody as an example, one can observe the character and overall shape or trajectory, hearing and feeling the contour (smoothly curving, continuous, disjunct, swirling, jagged, jutting, ascending, descending, level, undulating, combinations of these), sensing climaxes and tones which are emphasized by repetition or setting; the nature of the pitches (starting a melody on the root, third or fifth of a triad and the quality this lends to the beginning of a phrase or wherever it occurs, the presence or predominance of particular scale tones and their characteristics); intervals and how they affect the melody (large, small, mixed, dramatic leaps, careful consecutive steps, scale segments, skips, arpeggios, serpentine chromatics, predominance of particular intervals and their flavor); goal notes and "progress notes."

To explain the last two, goal notes are sensed as important arrival points, usually one or two at the most in a given phrase. I think of progress notes as significant landmarks toward and receding away from goal notes, marking the outline of directional movement, naturally more frequent in longer, complex phrases. In performance we need to feel the importance of these notes with an active sense of motion gravitating about them.

The intuiting of melodic highlights is a very revealing process which leads one deeply into the life of the phrase, the substance of musical matter, as one experiments with various versions to find the most instinctively satisfying form.

For an instrumentalist, singing a melody with one's own voice can bring it to life. One feels on the tongue and palate, in the throat, the lungs, each nuance, each leap—creating an intimate knowing which is necessary to interpret melody beautifully. We then transfer the contour to fingerpads which lovingly shape every bend, able now to sing and understand the song.

It is fascinating to study in contrapuntal passages how melodies interact—whether they move in parallel or contrary motion, what intervals they form conjointly, when they create dissonance and when consonance, how their individual high and low points relate—and also to enjoy the total effect of all the musical strands as they weave a tapestry of sound.

Rhythm

As far as rhythm is concerned, in brief, one could similarly study note values, patterns, similar/dissimilar, regularity, syncopation, the role of silence, complexity (two vs. three, etc.), comparing and contrasting rhythmic designs in different voices (as well as their composite rhythm), and character (galloping, dancey, solemn, funereal, strolling, epigrammatic). These characteristics are related to the meter—the nature and quantity of pulse and its organization in time—as well as *tempo* itself, two more areas we can fruitfully probe.

Rhythm, as much as melody, requires imagination to portray vibrantly. The dimension of time is a critical element in music, measured more specifically, more concretely, by a composer than by a dramatist or a poet, for whom time is also significant.

After quantifying it, a performer needs to *feel* a rhythm in his whole body, to sense its relation to his own pulse and breathing. We need to understand and enjoy its particular nature and project it with lively cadence, flexibility, point and sparkle to make it live. Dancing a rhythm around the room with one's entire body, head, torso, diaphragm, legs, feet, arms out to the fingertips will make it real. If you feel it moving in your very center, it will energize the music.

Harmony

To touch upon harmony, one could explore the relationship of harmony to melody (arpeggiated melodies that spell out harmonies, short scales that outline a chord, tones as consonant or dissonant with the current harmony), certain chords repeating, prevailing or acting as poles or as containers for other chords, noting basic progressions and observing how they and other more exotic progressions flavor the melody and define its color, differentiating such elements as rich chromaticism, pure triads, misty impressionism, shifting tonal centers, atonality, polytonality.

We dwell on each harmonic progression, repeating, listening, savoring the particular sound-quality and emotional suggestion of each chord and each change until we feel an intimate association, each becoming a familiar and special friend.

A knowledge of harmony is a tremendous boon to music study for both aesthetic appreciation and as an aide in memorizing. One or two concepts (f minor → C7) are so much easier to comprehend and remember than ten or twenty particular notes.

I enjoy increasingly listening to harmonic relationships as discrete and dynamic entities as I play and study a piece, recognizing how often melody is harmony-made-fluent by extension or embellishment, how intrinsic to the unfolding drama is the harmony, and how much one's understanding and memory of music is embodied in the harmony and enriched by it.

Texture

Texture too is an interesting matter to investigate. Is it open or closed, diffuse or concentrated and how is it distributed among the voices? Is it transparent, translucent or opaque, how much "light" shines through the voices (dappled, trellis-like) or how much spaciousness surrounds them. We can explore voice relationships (contrapuntal vs. homophonic, melody and accompaniment, chordal) and make comparisons with the texture of fabrics and threads (lacey, rough-woven, variegated, homogeneous).

Physical Thrust and Energy

The subject of physical thrust is a fascinating one, a bit less "factual," occupying a higher rung on that ladder of analysis we built. Our sense of the physical presence of an idea will be enhanced if we try to think in terms of such properties as shape, mass, density, speed, momentum, weight, length, breadth, texture. I find this a very stimulating way to examine music.

Thrust might be considered as a dimension generated by the motion of a musical idea through space and time, the energy both required and produced by this moving body. What impression does the phrase make on the space it penetrates, what is the nature of the imprint it makes on our consciousness?

To develop a sense of this aspect of music, it will help to become aware of a basic principle involving direction and effort. Just as it requires more work to climb a hill, a phrase or portion which ascends seems to express symbolically greater energy than one which descends. The latter will sound as if it is "giving in," resigned, bowing, succumbing, accepting, falling, whereas the former expresses an energetic stance, asserting itself, trying to overcome gravity, reaching, striving, growing, struggling, possibly even defiant, powerful, bold. This is not a hard and fast formula, but it is often found to operate and is helpful as a touchstone.

Of course the speed of ascent or descent, the intervals, rhythm, the voicing and texture, volume and range—indeed, the totality of the gesture will characterize each idea more richly and specifically. One will feel the greater energy involved in sharp, strong *staccatos* as opposed to fluid, unruffled *legato;* the activity stimulated by rapid sixteenth or thirty-second notes; the weight or deliberation lent to an idea by a series of half-note chords or the suspense created by relentless repetitions of tones, the massive strength of a sudden declaration of close position chords.

This awareness of physical shape and momentum has led us right into the realm of mood and imagery. Ideas will be observed to permeate a space like fingers of fog or spread like watercolors, to rocket up into the air, to march broadly, to hover, to weave their way like slender silver threads, etc.

Function, the Affinity of Musical Ideas for Each Other

Another dimension which is more elusive, but must be considered, is the *function* of a musical thought. Teachers can offer language to their students which will enable them to talk about music vividly with a functional basis and an imaginative flavor. Is an idea simply declarative, does it sound introductory, does it ask a question or offer an answer (open or closed); is it an invocation, an exclamation, announcement or pronouncement (attention getter), a reservoir of ideas, a generator, a connector or bridge, a conclusion (closing idea), an expansion or extension of a previous thought, a counter-proposal or alternative suggestion, a reworking, restatement or variant?

These qualities mostly suggest relationships with adjoining phrases, as one would expect, since music is a continuum, a narrative. We are examining the parts only to understand better and project the meaning of the whole. We can see how these perceptions lead naturally to a study of structure. If we begin to be aware of function (and thereby relationships) at the phrase level in this meaningful fashion, with personal receivers alert to musical language and punctuation, the extension of our study to larger forms will have more relevance. It will be rooted in the real affinity of musical ideas for each other.

This is a far from exhaustive list but perhaps it will suggest a productive, illuminating way of thinking about music as we practice it.

Character-Sensing

As one hears, analyzes, sorts out, befriends and enjoys the critical elements, an overall character begins to assert itself. A mood is felt, a message starts to speak. This is a unified and multidimensional experience. The particular faculties involved in the layering of perception are difficult to discern. The process is a function of our remarkable body-oneness. For a practiced musician, the tactile moulding of a phrase works so closely with the ear, the concrete information of the music and the emotions that one cannot separate the conscious from the unconscious aspects. Touch works to produce pleasure for the ear and the ear responds and evaluates. As a student, one must work to be certain this cycle of listening, sensing, evaluating and revising is occurring.

Stimulate Intuitive Responses by Considering Mood and "Message"

Although this character-sensing stage flows naturally out of the early fact-defining stage, and indeed is constantly interwoven with it, one must be aware of it and be sure that it happens. This means, for teachers, discussing character, mood, message with students, stimulating their own intuitive responses by offering an appropriate vocabulary, a sensing process and a thinking procedure. A teacher's ideas can act as a catalyst for theirs, suggesting rather than ordaining, so that a student's originality will be encouraged, start to blossom and later take shape with more experience and knowledge.

A performer may realize his own individual emotional response to an idea by trying to find words to describe that nonverbal but powerfully present message in the music. He needs to feel an identity with the emotions of each mood, a closeness to the music as well as a sure sense of self to be comfortable performing. This search is at once a delight for a musician and a vital link with the musical essence.

To be sure, we will not always be able to find words to match the moods. That is the wonder of music and so it should be. As Leonard Bernstein said masterfully in a discussion of musical meaning for young people:

> Sometimes we can name the things we feel, like joy or sadness or love or hate or peacefulness. But there are other feelings so deep and special that we have no words for them, and that's where music is especially marvelous. It names the feelings for us, only in notes instead of words.
>
> —(Bernstein 1962, 32)

And yet the attempt to articulate our response makes us aware of the boundless variety and power of music and connects us intimately to it.

We try to discern the emotion evoked by each idea in order to depict it in sound, to portray it with compelling color. Is an idea dignified, is it assertive—or perhaps bold, triumphant or pleading, retiring, serene, dreamy, mournful, poignant, reflective, meditative, angry, brave, searching, solemn, tragic, questioning? The shades of emotion will vary with each of us and what we bring to the music—personal history, daily moods, evolving periods of maturity.

This process is at the heart of the self-discovery and expansion music brings. As we stretch to comprehend and express the emotional content of every piece, every phrase, we find parts of ourselves therein. We make contact with and confirm the core of our feeling selves as we are sensitized by the music.

When I first begin to understand a musical idea I am often stirred by that special excitement one feels in the presence of something new and beautiful. It is like a bright light shining within me.

One of the greatest joys of living with music is the return to a piece well-studied in the past, an old friend, to discover new levels of meaning, more intensity of emotion or even new emotions corresponding to our heightened capacity to understand and feel. We experience journal writing in a similar way, as a parallel process of inner exploration and affirmation through heightened awareness of our responses to *all* of life, the realm of music and beyond.

A fine performer will enter the mood of a piece completely, indeed, will give himself to the experience of the music. When there is emotional involvement, music is charged with vitality, with electrifying energy, and the performer feels a deep and stabilizing connection with the music.

Entering the Emotional Current

The depth and consistency of emotional commitment during performance depends on *how one enters a piece* as well as how one has studied.

We have already described some features of that moment of peace prior to performing. One's attitude toward the imminent experience is so important. Let us add now the crucial element of diving deeply into the emotional current at the outset.

Seated comfortably and peacefully with our instrument before starting, we hone in on the mood and spirit of the opening phrase by hearing it vividly in the mind's ear and feeling it fully. Our antennae alert to receive the meaning, to imagine the color, to sense the emotional content, we focus on this rich reality with all of our being. It is a complete world that draws us in.

The intensity with which we hear and feel the beginning of the piece will determine the level of entry, and the level of entry is critical. That first phrase can be like an open tunnel into the center of the piece. If you really climb into it, wholeheartedly, it will carry you into the deepest levels of musical experience— into the primary energy flow, a river of feelings and moods, the emotional currents that course in the most profound musical communication.

In this expressive state one is both filled with the music and given to the music—indeed, one becomes the music. Continuing to feel the developing moods of the piece with total commitment, there is no room for me-thoughts. The focus is on the music, not the self.

One might practice conjuring up the spirit of a piece (sometimes even away from your instrument) as well as practicing the manner of beginning just described. We should devote time to this as we do to other elements of study. Practice hearing it in your head, practice feeling the mood, practice bringing yourself back to the sound if your attention strays, practice staying *inside* the music. Practice how one feels during performance, deep in the emotional flow. It should be a familiar state, not a surprise when you perform. More on practicing performance later.

Clearly this entry technique works only in conjunction with the whole process of study. Each phase helps us in a particular way but is, by itself, insufficient as preparation.

HOW-TO-DO-IT

The Business-Like Stage of Learning

In a sense, we have been discussing the "what," and now we move on to the "how to." We begin by emphasizing the importance of the most fundamental level, what I call (especially for those spontaneous students who tend to neglect it) the business-like stage of learning.

Scholarly Approach to the Score

We have an unequivocal responsibility to the composer to learn the facts of his music first, to be true to the score. One might say those little black dots and lines on the page present a puzzle to be solved. The composer has encoded, in a language we must decipher, the sounds he heard in his ear or in his mind's ear. There is a great gap between a page of print and the vibrant reality of musical sound. To even begin to imagine and then to reproduce what the composer heard, we need at the very least to be scholarly in our approach to his notation. We must read meticulously every basic marking in the score (pitch, rhythmic values, rests, phrasing, repeats, *staccato, legato*, etc.) and be alert to all interpretative indications as well (dynamics, accents, *tempi*, pacing, mood).

One needs also to study the customs of the period to understand the *implications* of the notation as well as what to our twentieth century eyes and ears may seem like omissions. For example, the lack of phrase marks in Baroque scores by no means indicates continuous *legato* or uniform *nonlegato*. It was assumed that the experienced performer (who was often the composer himself) would understand the musical style and performance practice well enough to provide appropriate phrasing himself, exercising his own taste and judgment to make a personal contribution as well.

How Much Analysis for Young Children?

It might be mentioned at this point that the amount and degree of technical analysis should be appropriate to the age and level of the student. The very youngest will be absorbing musical information primarily through the senses (hearing, touching, feeling, seeing) by imitation and, to use an apt but abused expression, holistically, with the playfulness and curiosity natural to this early developmental stage. The Suzuki Method recognizes this early youthful attribute and employs listening, imitation and group experiences in a nurturing atmosphere, emulating the natural environmental features of language learning as a model.

Sensory Learning

John Holt[1] called these youngsters "little scientists or explorers" rather than the usual "sponges," pointing out their relentless and delighted sensory experimentation with the world around them. Watch a toddler, all alone, building with blocks and you will see him studying physics—learning principles of balance, gravity, size, weight, proportion, design. Entirely by touch, sight, intuition, trial and error, he is dealing with the basic realities of the physical world—and aesthetics as well. Early learning must acknowledge and flow naturally with this marvelous curiosity, independent ability and sensory delight, but this is a huge topic in itself.

Nuts and Bolts

Although it is sound itself, with its patterns and spirited energy that has the overwhelming appeal for the very young, they will enjoy figuring out what makes the music tick, as they might curiously explore the inner workings of an old clock or radio, discovering the nuts and bolts of music. They can distinguish melodies; they thoroughly enjoy rhythmic clapping games and identifying tunes from the rhythm alone. They can recognize chords as such and hear when they change or "want to" change with new melody notes.

They will also enjoy detecting when notes repeat or go uphill or downhill, or sound long or short, ending with a long tail or a crisp pop. They can compare and imitate rhythms and count the silent places and notice whenever a familiar melody or motif or instrument returns. Such listening activities and many others can be encouraged in friendly groups as well as in private lessons. They will help, in addition to laying an aural foundation for the future analytic approach, to focus musical education on *sensitive hearing*, the most vital skill of the fully matured artist.

---

[1] Holt Lecture, Escondido, California, July 16, 1984.

The musical faculties of youngsters are often underestimated. I have been aware of this since 1957 when as a college senior I enjoyed teaching preschoolers in a musical nursery in my Cambridge studio. I found as my intuition had predicted, that these young children could learn almost anything if it were presented accessibly, with a pleasure that reflected their own natural delight in learning.

Seeds for a Way of Thinking About Music

Young children can make rudimentary observations about form, such as hearing in ABA form the A as "home," the B as "vacation" and the satisfying return to home again, or hearing a musical question and answer. Using imagery in such comprehensible allusions to form will heighten awareness of structural parts and their relationships. Thus we early plant the seeds for a *way of thinking about music* which can evolve gradually through the years.

We also need to root, from the very beginning, the concept of practicing *parts* of the music in order to learn thoroughly and systematically. It is helpful to make up imaginative names for discernible parts and accustom children to repeating little bits and sections of music through enjoyable games (using abacus, charts, score-keeping) while listening for improvement in tone, articulation, dynamics, etc.

First Goals of Score Study: Right Notes, Rhythm, Phrasing, Good Fingering

Returning now, with older students and adults, to that early factual stage of training a scholarly attention to the score, our first goals are the right notes, right rhythm and right phrasing, and here I like to include good fingering. I don't say right fingering, because fingering needs to be adapted to each person's hands and fingers and we sometimes alter the editor's suggestion. But we must consider it from the very beginning so that a musician develops the habit of observing those numbers and relating to them physically. Although not a fact designated by the composer, comfortable fingering is crucial to setting the kinesthetic response in our muscles and it must be treated with the most respectful attention.

It is extremely difficult and time-consuming to unlearn and replace fingering and those first vivid impressions have a way of lasting. They have been known to resurface persistently months later. Using appropriate fingering from the start and using the same fingering consistently is a fundamental requirement that cannot be overemphasized both for digesting a piece thoroughly and preparing for performance.

Separate and Develop Skills

At this point in learning a given phrase, we might break down the tone-producing tools of our instrument into any workable units that can be studied and refined separately. We can thus isolate and perfect technical skills as appropriate to the interpretation of the phrase.

For example, the string player can work on the fine art of bowing alone, giving all of his attention to perfecting the subtlety of his bow strokes. The precision of left hand placement and weight for intonation and tone quality can also be practiced carefully and separately, as well as vibrato technique.

Pianists will now be working primarily with separate hands, focusing on achieving accuracy, fine tone and physical comfort with that hand (at times including multiple voices) just as a performer on a solo melodic instrument would devote his total person to his "part." We study in detail the musical contribution of each hand in each section, devoting the whole brain and all faculties to understanding, appreciating and processing the message of each. The better we hear each voice, the better we will hear the whole.

Although the fine tuning of tone production happens in later stages, we always need to be aware of the beauty of our sound, listening for a basic fine quality, a standard of warmth, resonance and clarity now even as a working model.

We want to develop an inner concept of beautiful tone—a *true* sound in the mind's ear—and continually refine this aural image as a reference point. Listening sensitively and working to improve tone quality adds intense engagement and vitality to practice time and increases a student's sense of autonomy.

Repetition: Enjoying, Evaluating and Improving

We repeat each thought, hoping to make the next repetition more successful than the last, until it is as beautiful as it can be "for that day," a better goal than ten times or fifteen times—or 50 or 60—because it engages the musician in active listening; in planning, evaluating and improving with each repetition rather than drearily and mechanically accumulating the required number of repeats. Some young children need and enjoy a specified number of repeats, and often relish the challenge of topping yesterday's number, but we still emphasize sensitive listening for improvement.

If the phrase is not satisfactory to the ear, one needs to determine exactly where and why. We may need to enter the phrase more deeply by isolating and polishing a smaller troublesome bit—perhaps a large intervallic leap or a difficult slur or an odd rhythmic group or a challenging sixteenth note run.

It seems that we learn better when we *enjoy* what we are doing and the contrary is also true—that tension seems to inhibit progress. I believe we also deter anxiety by allowing ourselves to enjoy. While repeating passages, we want to cultivate an openness to the beauty of the music, actively seeking to relish its particular qualities and finding increasing pleasure as the passage improves. We also need, not to berate, but to be kind to ourselves and believe in our ability as we work, maintaining an open feeling that welcomes experience.

A problem solving approach is helpful—with a reasonable concentration on the task at hand, patience and persistence. If we are working on a challenging section, we can take delight in transforming this "problem" into something beautiful.

An active brain trains the body. If we practice mechanically, turning off the thinking self or letting the mind wander, our muscles may revert to habit and play the passage "the old way." If we listen carefully, tuned into and appreciating the precise nature of the sound, constantly evaluating and planning anew as we repeat, we keep improving.

Slowly and Steadily

It is important to emphasize playing slowly and steadily at this stage—enabling us to hear details clearly and planting "in the bones" a regular pulse, exact rhythms and precisely equal like-valued notes. The musical ideas come to life with correct rhythmic proportions even at a slow *tempo* and indeed impart a special sense of integrity and character in this measured, deliberate and sturdy rendering.

When we are certain of an accurate, technically apt and understanding reading of the score, we begin gradually to increase our speed, continuing however to work regularly at several *tempi* from slow to performance level, (especially useful is moderate speed) in order to achieve total control. A musician really has mastery only when he can play a piece well at numerous speeds, including slow.

Stopping to Correct

This is the stage in which we stop and correct if necessary, to be distinguished from that later stage when we are working for continuity above all and need to keep the flow and momentum of the "story line." Both kinds of practice are necessary in their places, but should be clearly separated in our minds.

We shouldn't allow lapses to go unattended or uncorrected now when we are working to establish the correct patterns in our system. If we repeat a phrase with an error, we are *learning* that error, or if we repeatedly play irregularly we are learning irregularity. If we continually err in different ways each time, we are practicing too fast or the music is too advanced for our current ability. Repeated stumbles in the same passage deserve specific technical analysis. (See sections on physical preparation in Chapter VI.)

If we play a phrase with the intent of stopping to study and correct *any* flaw we will play with a higher expectation level and more alertness, thereby achieving a higher level of accuracy and beauty. Clearly in subsequent stages we need to work for continuity as well as polish and performance readiness.

Some children enjoy scoring themselves from one to ten for each repetition, an Olympic "ten" representing the ideal beautiful sound, and they listen to their sound remarkably well when playing this game. They are also quite fair in their judgments.

Larger Sections with Separate Hands on Piano

Pianists can gain much benefit from practicing larger sections as well as phrases with separate hands. Concentration is thus more intensely focused on the one hand, musically and technically, before expanding to include both. There is a logic to this technique since one hand will often play a consistent role such as solo melody, chordal or arpeggiated accompaniment or counter theme and will receive thorough scrutiny this way. In addition, physical maneuvers inherent to the part will get extended treatment and greater control.

Voice Integrity

One can imagine each hand as a part for string or wind instrument (or two or more) to understand the musical wholeness and total attention it requires for complete comprehension and control. Then, when the parts are played together, each will bear the integrity of an entire person's effort and will contribute richly to the total result, the performer well-prepared to hear and project the true nature of each part.

In first lessons on a new piece, and continuing until basic standards are met, it is useful for a teacher to hear the hands separately and fairly slowly. One can thus examine more carefully the accuracy, fingering and fine details. It also assures that the music is indeed practiced this way and reinforces careful study habits.

Value of Left Hand Study

There is particular value in studying the left hand alone with great care and appreciation—both for understanding the music and performance security. When we listen to music our ears tend to hear top lines foremost and lower voices secondarily, thus etching them less sharply in our memory. Most often memory lapses involve the left hand part so a greater conscious effort to learn it is in order.

Yet the musical motivation is even more telling. Left hand parts often contain the harmony, which we may well regard as the heart of the music. Indeed, the progression of harmonies is germane to expressivity in music; it determines the flux of tension and release more conclusively than any other element as well as the particular perfume or coloration lent to a single melody note. Harmony is most often responsible for those transcendent moments of beauty in music that seem to have a special power to move us, to alter us profoundly.

Thus the left hand part often provides clues to phrase division (through harmonic "grammar") as well as signaling important emotive changes. It may also contain hidden melodies, buried in the voicing of chords or in periodic bass tones. These are more easily discovered when the left hand role is carefully examined alone. When beautifully sustained or sensitively inflected, as appropriate, these subtle threads add much richness to the musical tapestry.

Of course, there may occur a more forthright supportive or contrapuntal melody in the bass or even a solo voice. Here too the musician's left hand will benefit, in this unaccustomed role, from extra attention to developing a fine singing tone.

The bass portion of the music is often responsible for intense rhythmic urges or pulsing effects. Feeling them purely, in isolation, helps to focus and concentrate the energy of these impulses, delivering an urgent motor force when assimilated into the music. If we strive to make the left hand part a thing of beauty in itself, the artistry of the whole will be enhanced.

Establish Geographic Units in the Mind Early

In practicing these phrases, and later with larger sections or "paragraphs," it is essential to start and stop at the same point with each repetition, so that geographic units are mentally established early and reinforced during the whole preparation period. This builds a very solid sense of the structure and aids tremendously in performance.

The size of a working section will depend on the musical material and the length of the piece and may contain more than one phrase. This is entirely personal and variable but it should be a workable length, short enough to constitute a reasonable memorizing unit.

Internalize Music Soon

As soon as possible too, one might begin to alternate looking and not looking at the page with each repeat. Thus, we internalize and digest the musical material early, transforming it from the external printed code on the page into a meaningful inner sequence of sound-ideas, making use of the familiar "handles" of musical detail from our analysis to help us memorize. This alternation of visual aide with memory assures greater accuracy as we are continually returning to the information source, comparing and verifying our effort.

When we play with score we are reminded of *what the composer wants;* when we play without score we discover *what we know* of his intention.

If a weak point is revealed during a memory-try, we immediately consult the score and restudy that segment with greater precision and detail. Gradually we attempt larger numbers of memory-tries before returning again to the score.

At this point, and even later during practice performances, a mistake or stumble can be considered a gift. The music is telling you "practice me here." One should be delighted to have this directive to respond to. The children love to hear (and repeat) "a goof is a gift."

Even after memorization is solid, one keeps the score at hand or on the rack, much of the time. Increasingly, as the music is internalized, one practices performance with no book standing on the rack. This liberation is as essential as the scholarly returning to the score for authenticity.

The Suzuki approach aims for a very deep and unconscious internalization of the music by ear, through repeated hearing of records or tapes of the music being studied, future and review pieces as well, postponing visual use of score until aural learning is established. Some traditional teachers too have for many years recommended listening to both live concerts and recordings, also comparing various artists' interpretations as an excellent means of honing one's own. Suzuki adds to this the notion of intensive listening from the very beginning, indeed from the cradle, to initiate an aural orientation and absorb the music naturally, developing an ear for tone quality, phrasing and style.

It should be noted that repeated listening to fine recordings of your performance piece will contribute immeasurably to your confidence, thoroughly implanting knowledge of the music in your brain and reinforcing your study and practice.

Integrating Skills—the Full Shape of the Music

The moment of returning to the phrase with separate skills intact brings an important satisfaction: by integrating the elements, the messages, of both hands, or of pitch and breath control, one arrives at the full shape of the music, feeling more emotional connection with it (although we continue to work also with separate hands or single skills as necessary even in later stages for securing technique and memory or refining nuance).

We also can say we have completed the basic fact-finding stage when we perceive the parts relating as a whole. We can now hear the harmonic progressions in entirety, appreciate the counterpoint of voices and the full richness of the texture. We can better plumb the meaning of each phrase, determine its character and work now to delineate that character with appropriate color—dynamic shaping and contrast, variations in tone, touch, pedaling, breathing and timing—building ourselves into the music as we make these detailed interpretive decisions. As our energies turn to the full import of the music, we can feel assured that our careful preparation of each skill brings accuracy and validity to the whole.

Exactly when pianists begin to study hands together will vary with the individual and the piece. With most students, as soon as the whole of a short piece or a reasonably long section of a larger piece is digested and fluent with each hand, we start to play together. Depending on a student's needs, maturity and stage of development, we might start hands together as each phrase is secured with individual hands.

Analogy to Painting

A word on appropriate color—the visual analog is so illuminating here, as we experiment with various effects, seeking to derive a palette of sounds to paint an *aural* scene, using the rich resources and techniques of our instrument to develop musical character.

We dip into the vast spectrum of dynamic hues from *fff* to *ppp*, to find our volume levels. We explore the range of touches—our brush strokes—from a full flowing *cantabile legato* to a crisp dry pointillist *staccato*. With careful timing we can create space to highlight an ensuing sound or surround it with a plain expressive canvas of silence. Pianists can apply a very liquid pedal to saturate the texture, blend smoothly with syncopated pedaling or merely moisten and lightly sustain with a deft fluttering pedal. This stage of discovering character and employing color to paint it is as essential to the recreative process as the fundamental fact-finding period.

Descriptive Mode Aids Teaching and Interpreting

We all know that visual and emotional descriptions of musical events have been overdone at times—they are prone to grow "purple." Certainly we should avoid overdramatizing or substituting imagery for clear thinking about musical happenings, but we must also be careful not to slip into academic rejection of the descriptive mode. It is a true aid in teaching and interpreting, helping to awaken the imagination, to personalize the response, to effect an emotional commitment. All of these human faculties are needed if we are to recreate the art with the intensity and richness imparted by the composer.

STRUCTURE, PRINCIPLES OF COMPOSITION AND REFINING

Structure: Relationships of Musical Ideas

The next level of study carries us up to relationships among phrases, sections and the larger structure, casting further light on each thought even as we perceive the whole with more lucidity. Having identified, characterized and colored an idea, we now try to learn what the composer does with it; exactly what changes and how it changes as we hear the next phrase (melody, rhythm, harmony, etc.); what remains the same; what are the subtle grammatic relationships suggested by the evolving material?

In discussing the function of musical ideas (e.g. introduction, extension, bridge, conclusion), we have already considered the implied relationships. We go on now to explore these musical facts further—the nature of this relating and the composer's means of achieving continuity.

Does he use repetition? This is the most frequent and favored device: he likes the idea, he says it again to be sure we hear it and remember it, often going on to develop and extend it (Bernstein's engaging observation: "one, two and away we go!") or does he introduce a new thought? Do we hear an antecedent-consequent relationship—statement and counter-statement or question and answer? Does he use variation technique, fragmentation and alteration, regeneration, sequence, inversion (reflection), diminution, augmentation, accumulation, reduction, retrograde motion, "tail" development? As we sense the nature of idea-evolution, we experiment with appropriate color changes.

"Paragraphs"

We begin to consider larger sections or paragraphs and notice how a series of ideas comes to partial rest or an important cadence, completing a portion of the composer's argument or narrative. Later in Chapter V, as we describe the securing for performance of a support system of starting places, we will see the virtue of our consistent work with these basic units we have identified (starting and stopping at the same spots as we repeat the building blocks) and now the location of the larger portions that grow logically out of the parts.

Just as the thoughts relate systematically to one another within these larger regions, we will be relating the *starting points* of each thought within the *same areas,* using cues of harmony, register, pitch, disposition, etc., to group them intelligibly.

We now practice these paragraphs as whole units in addition to the phrase-units, getting a feeling for the larger picture. It is important at this point to grow comfortable with the flow of the musical stream, thoroughly training our muscles and neurons in *continuity*, accustoming our whole system to the logical joining of these secured units.

Formal Scheme

We begin then to observe the general relationships of paragraphs to one another in an effort to arrive at a sense of the whole formal scheme. Are new ideas introduced, previous ideas developed, retreated or set in a new context? Do new ideas derive from earlier material in any way? Is the pacing similar or altered; the meter, note values, voicing, texture, register? Is there a shift in tonality or attitude toward tonality, or a change in the pace of harmonic rhythm? Do these new elements denote a regional contrast suggestive of a major area in the overall structural design?

Unique Structures; Conventional Expectations and Idiosyncratic Choices

As we ponder the question of form, it is important to move initially from the particular facts of a piece to any conclusions about its overall design, rather than to superimpose an expected or preconceived shape upon it. That is, to appreciate each work of art with its own idiosyncratic features, personality and shape. It might bear a unique form or lean more toward a generic design such as Sonata-Allegro, Rondo, Theme and Variations, or ABA (ternary form) but even such forms should not be perceived as recipes for music writing or as molds into which ideas are poured.

Rather, in finely wrought pieces, form interacts organically with the materials, evolving out of them or suggesting pathways for transformation that result in lively variants even in traditional settings. Part of the excitement of the whole idea of structure in art is the electricity of tension between conventional expectations and idiosyncratic choices.

It is most enlightening to observe the musical usages and techniques of *this* composer in *this* piece, moving only then to an estimation of the form and then to the fascinating and revealing matter of historic parallels with other works, evolution of a composer's attitude toward form, and comparisons of composers and periods. Each work of art deserves a particular analysis, the immediacy and liveliness of one's spontaneous musical response as well as the breadth and depth of interpretive vision that comes from historical perspective and musicological awareness.

Value of Studying Form

As a performer, one cannot overvalue a deep knowledge of form and constant sensitivity to it—both in the work one is learning and music at large. When there is clarity of structural understanding, one projects a sense of coherence, of orderliness in the telling of the story. The musician's depiction of each musical thought will be subtly colored by his awareness of its place in the larger plan, its way of relating to previous and subsequent ideas. The music is thus rendered with deeply rooted meaning in addition to appropriateness, clean passages, expressivity.

Josef Hofmann said, "study forms until you *feel* them!" In other words, take this knowledge to the deepest level so that it becomes intuitive, so that you are subconsciously attuned to architecture as you perform. Your resultant delight in the nuance of form will bring zest to your interpretation and performance.

Principles of Composition

Further depth is achieved by considering artistic principles of composition—the less visible organic formations one can discern within the musical contours. Why do the parts work so well together? Hidden in the fabric of the music are such integrative elements as unity and variety, economy of means, contrast, parallelism, transformation, accumulation and reduction of forces, graduation (gradual change)—involved with building intensity over a long period or dissolving, fading to silence or *ppp*—regularity and irregularity, tension and release.

Tension and Release: the Primary Flux

The last principle, tension and release, is a particularly interesting aspect to contemplate, corresponding in both fine detail and broader dimension to the primary flux of life itself. Music reflects both the rhythm of the earth's rotation and the fluctuation of human lives; the alternation of summer and winter, day and night, light and dark, joy and grief, knowing and leaving, intensity and calm, activity and rest—the seasons of the universe and the seasons of our hearts.

Musical tension and release can be found in the microcosm in such events as the resolution of dissonance to consonance and in its larger form as segments of relative stress dissolve to calm or in the dissipation of a driving rhythmic pattern or the sequential appearance of entire contrasting movements—a fiery *agitato* followed by a meditative *andante.*

Catharsis from Parallels to Ebb and Flow of Life

Indeed, the inimitable catharsis of the musical experience must depend partly on this correspondence to the ebb and flow of the human condition as well as on feeling in one's own body all the varied emotions inherent in the changing sounds.

Refining and Polishing

The next phase in the preparation of a piece for performance involves refining and polishing. The facts are known, the characterization and coloring have continued to develop through the stage of clarifying the structure and now one is absorbed by the finer facets of the art—in terms both of interpretation and the securing of technical control. Physical proficiency is obviously a central issue which will be discussed to an appropriate degree in a later segment.

We now attend to matters of fine-tuning such as interpretive nuance (in further honing message, mood and sound)—details of timing, pacing, dramatic highlighting, tonal and dynamic subtleties; touch, precision in balance, full use of the magic of pedaling, settling of *tempi*, richer characterization of ideas through overall architectural considerations—location, proportion of intensity levels, dynamic scale in larger regions and movements as well as subsections.

During this refining process we are securing the sensory-motor skills—that is, getting the music deeply "into our muscles" as well as setting the fine details. We still work in sections but include more complete performances, aiming for continuity and an increasingly familiar perception of the whole, tactilely, aurally, emotionally and intellectually. In sections we emphasize integrated skills but also persist, pianists for example, in individual hand work as appropriate, for technical and memory purposes.

Alternate Inner Ear with Actual Playing

At this stage and even earlier, the technique of alternating actual playing of a phrase with imagining it is extremely helpful and stimulating, producing remarkable improvement. If one can hear in the inner ear an ideal, most beautiful version, one is more likely then to be able to reproduce it in real sound, developing that quintessential faculty of *keen, real listening to oneself,* to one's actual sound, as we seek to match this ideal. One's imagination is unencumbered by habitual body movements or the current state of one's tone production in the passage. One is not then at the mercy of one's fingers, imitating one's own previous rendering still fresh in the ear, but constantly striving toward the finest aesthetic one can imagine. The inner ear is thus conductor to the fingers (children enjoy this image), having a plan, an intended sound which the fingers as orchestral members will learn to realize.

Personal Imagery and Concentration

Using our imagination to the fullest in this stage as we refine our interpretation, developing a rich personal imagery, has the effect of anchoring the music at the deepest subconscious levels and providing a meaningful inner vision during performance—specific emotions, verbal and visual images where natural and appropriate, and everywhere an intense and abstract becoming of the phrase itself which cannot translate into words, an expansion of our spirit to fill the music.

It is the actual experiencing, "in our bones," of hours of this kind of thoughtful, contemplative and creative practice that will further secure an effective foundation for *concentration,* a vital element in performance. We care, we interact and bond with the music at the deepest emotive levels and will be therefore less easily distracted. Our grounding will not be shallow; there is much material on which to concentrate. The performer's senses will be informed and enriched by inner necessity, a compelling relatedness.

It is not enough to advise a student to concentrate during performance. Musicians can be guided to create a full, rich inner world in which to dwell— something to concentrate *on.* They need to be very busy recreating this world of beautiful sounds—strong and richly singing here, delicate and sparkling like distant stars elsewhere, bold, assertive chords, lacey arpeggios; focusing and employing one's personal energy intensively so that it won't filter away.

SOME INTERPRETIVE CONSIDERATIONS

Interpretation is a vast world that develops from the totality of one's life experiences and faculties. Here we will simply sketch lightly some considerations.

In a sense, interpretation may be thought of as a distillation, through the medium of the music, of a performer's knowledge, judgment, taste and intuitions.

Historical Epoch

Each piece exists against the backdrop of its historical epoch (social behavior, politics, religion, aesthetics, etc.), musical styles and customs—including instruments, "sound-ideals," preferred forms and traditions and the composer's life and total works. The more one studies these facts (as best they can be recreated today), the more richly documented and authentic will be one's interpretation. We can read history, letters, autobiography, biography and fiction to steep ourselves in the real atmosphere of the times. One can search out the art and architecture of the period, read the poetry, see the drama. One can go to contemporaneous treatises for insights into performance practice during the composer's lifetime and also to more recent musicological reports for the stimulation of scholarly analysis.

Judgment and Taste

Judgment and taste will be developed by broad and deep experiences with music, especially by much exposure to distinguished performance, by sensitive listening to the variety of possible interpretations in order to detect why and how they work, what makes them either convincing or less persuasive to *our* ears. We thus accumulate criteria to apply to our own efforts and develop the ability to assess and evaluate our own interpretative ideas.

Intuition and Personality

Finally, one's intuition and personality are crucial in determining the degree and proportion of musical elements appropriate to each piece. For this, C.P.E. Bach suggests we need "insight into the character of the piece" (Dorian 1942, 163). Exactly how fast should it be, how loud, how soft, how *staccato*, how *legato?* For these decisions we need to be emotionally tuned-in to the heart and drive of the music, at one with the mood—hearing, feeling and projecting the message, one's imagery rooted in a real response to the sound. Here too creative imagination enters in, as we build a persuasive total picture of the piece, beautiful in its parts, proportions and inter-relationships—a plan for the whole which works on every level.

Pacing, Phrasing and Volume

We need to sense the pacing necessary for an idea to express itself fully. Some music seems to surge with a special vitality at a certain right *tempo*, while other music seems capable of speaking at many different *tempi.*

We must be careful not to overburden a thought with elaborate phrasing, neither should we neutralize it with bland phrasing. Good phrasing should realize and support the basic shape and thrust of a musical idea, highlighting rather than detracting from the goal notes. Our chosen effects must convey the mood, elucidate the nature of each idea, affirm the intent of the composer.

We need to modulate our volume to suit the intensity of the emotion and the dimensions of the work. Here too, years of experience with music will develop the musicianship necessary to sense these elements but one can enhance the skills with ear training, harmonic and contrapuntal studies, analysis and, above all, focused and intelligent listening to ourselves and others. One can train the ears to be more sensitive to intervals, to chord inversions and harmonic progressions.

Study Music for Other Instruments

It is also extremely helpful to hear and study music for other instruments—symphonic, operatic, vocal, keyboard, chamber music. A pianist will benefit vastly from learning the ways of a second instrument—a string or wind instrument or voice. The infusion of a fresh regard for line, *legato, cantabile* and breathing will help reveal the piano's capacity to sing warmly and richly as well as engender sensitivity to phrasing through first hand experience with real breathing or bowing.

Similarly, string and wind players could enrich their harmonic and contrapuntal understanding by studying a keyboard instrument, enhancing their sense of interplay with accompanists and ensemble groups.

Interpretive Ideas

Some specific interpretive ideas to keep in mind will follow.

Be alert to characterize and differentiate themes and thematic areas, noticing contrast of texture, key, register, melodic shape, rhythmic pattern, etc., and clearly define the particular nature of each. It sometimes helps to personify a theme as an imaginary character in an opera, with vivid human attributes.

Be keen to discover melody wherever it occurs and project it songfully, in proportion to its relative importance in the total texture. "Climb into" the melody and fully experience its every rise and fall. To feel this sensation of being inside every note of a melody, imagine that you are inside the tram of a roller coaster—that, indeed you *must* go up when it goes up and come down when it comes down. You need to care about and partake of each and every note even as you feel committed to the overall contour and message of the melody. Something *inside* you must climb up that sixth and descend that minor second.

This is indispensable in slow movements, where *tempo* and note-length challenge our ability to sustain the tensility of the line throughout an entire idea. It is your compelling inner awareness of the suspense that will maintain it.

You might perceive each note as a word in a story, where every word is essential to the meaning of a thought. Telling a story with occasional words omitted makes the point well. Similarly, we need to hear and participate emotionally in every note of *every* musical idea, not only in melody.

Always notice moving voices and bring them out against the backdrop of stationary voices. Be sensitive to *motion* in general, to forward direction, to progress from one place to another. Music exists in time and this dimension is its very essence.

Feel the pulse with intensity; it is as important as one's skeleton. But be sure it is similarly *inside* the body of your music, not exposed obviously on the outside.

Let your phrases arch and soar without being nailed down on each first beat of a measure. The meter should be felt as an internal structural mechanism.

Make use of meaningful *rubato* with an appreciation for rhythmic elasticity, only after determining note values with precision. Notice when a motor rhythmic drive is called for or an expansive, leisurely stroll or a measured, deliberate pace or a broad sense of each note filling its space and time to the fullest measure.

Sense moods and work to learn how to project them—using appropriate tone, touch, dynamics, breathing, pedaling (for coloring as well as prolonging), with your ear as the essential guide to your foot.

Maintain emotional continuity, permitting yourself to be vulnerable to nuance. Stay inside the music—one with its changing spirit. Be aware of points of repose and excitement, building climaxes and fading energy. Look for the high point (or points) and low points as well and plan your degrees of intensity and dynamic levels appropriately, designing an artistic and persuasive whole.

Cultivate a variety of touches and sounds from sparkling or pearl-like scale tones to an intense, full, rich *cantabile* with attention to the many different stages of *legato* and *staccato* technique, *portamento*, *nonlegato*, detached.

In your search for varied tone qualities, consider the diverse timbres of other instruments and imagine a particular instrument with a corresponding range singing a melodic line, trying to emulate the nature of that sound on your instrument. Various textures will suggest analogies with human voices or instrumental duos, wind or string quartets or trios, chamber orchestra, full orchestra, etc. One's imagination will be stimulated and interpretation will be enhanced by an attempt to fulfill the parallel on your piano or harp, to become the suggested sonority. One will then be moved to experiment further with new touches and attacks and timings to produce an as-yet unimagined kind of sound which will result in a broader spectrum of sonorities in your music making.

Elusive Passages

To be entirely realistic, you will find some passages, movements and pieces which evade understanding quite persistently. Some will open up after repeated exploration, perhaps with several intervening years of musical and emotional maturation. But the process of trying, the experimenting with many possible combinations of color and timing as you attempt to recreate a passage convincingly is an education in itself. Listening to many fine artists will be a significant help along this road to discovering your own empathic sense of the music.

CHAPTER **V**

A LIBERATING SYSTEM—THE PSYCHOLOGICAL REALM

PERFORMANCE STRATEGY

System of Starting Points

The rich detail and associations we have thus far built will help us feel intimately involved with each musical moment, focused and concentrating. Moreover, we will feel peaceful in performance with the knowledge of a reliable support system.

Woven into the polishing stage is the all-important process of securing a system of starting points within a clear structural framework and learning *how to use* this mental map you carry along as you travel through your piece. With the description of this system and its salutary effect on the entire interactive process of learning and performing, we clearly enter the realm of the psychological, and we can see how the cognitive preparation merges with the psychological.

Memorize Starting Points in Logical Formal Groupings

Part of our daily practice will include playing and memorizing the starting places themselves in sequence, grouping them in patterns according to formal design so they make sense, naming each mentally to emphasize the logic of their relationships—for example, key relationships such as A major high followed by A major low or f minor theme in RH followed by f minor theme in LH and closing idea in A flat, each of which could be abbreviated for easiest mental recall as:

A hi/ A lo

f RH/ f LH/ clos. A$\flat$.

Range (widespread or concentrated), octave disposition, scale degrees, or thematic treatment could all provide similar handles for brief and focused identification. We need to know each starting point as well as we know the beginning of the piece, even *as well as we know our names* in order to develop the necessary instant retrieval.

We repeat a half or whole measure or so of the start of each section, followed immediately by the other starting places within the larger structural group or paragraph of three or four, studying them thoroughly in sequence each day, until one instantly calls to mind the next.

We study and compare *similar* starting points, especially noting their differences and similarities specifically in terms of theme, harmony, register, structural location, etc.,—a most significant preventive measure since these can be vulnerable spots in performance.

We work assiduously on these geographical landmarks, overlearning, if you will, until a quite lucid skeletal scheme has taken shape, the piece "in a nutshell" to complement the broad-based and detailed knowledge we are also achieving.

This work with starting points will only have meaning if the sections they represent have been thoroughly digested as structural units, analytically and technically, continually reinforced by daily practice.

Learning to Use Starting Points; A Reliable Strategy for Performance

A crucial next step is to practice *using* the starting points successfully, first for yourself and gradually creating more challenging performance conditions, until you are certain of a reliable strategy for handling lapses in performance.

As well as the sectional and starting point practice already described, one should daily rehearse complete performances, including walking "on stage," imagining a waiting audience (all the better if you feel some shivers of excitement), bowing, sitting peacefully at the bench, centering your body and thoughts, feeling the spiritual elevation we have described, hearing your music and feeling its mood, gracefully approaching your instrument, entering the emotional flow intensely and then performing as though for an audience, without stopping for corrections, feeling a oneness with the mood of the piece and aiming for a polished, deeply-felt and *continuous* performance. This practice of continuity should be clearly distinguished from segmented practice where stopping to correct and study is as vital to the learning process as continuing is to the performing mode.

We feel the comfort of sailing along past each familiar landmark (starting point) as the music unfolds. If a lapse of any sort should occur we are hardly chagrined but rather grateful, even delighted, for this safe, protected opportunity to practice using our starting points, and grateful as well for this revealing detection of weak points in memory or technique, now pinpointed for more intensive study. Remember, the slip is a *gift* telling you "practice me here!"

Instantly, Calmly Resume Flow After Any Lapse

If we can immediately pick up the musical thread where we dropped it, we do so, but if not, we instantly resume the flow at the very next starting point—in either case maintaining a calm facial and body expression, not emitting any goshes or whoopses, letting hand fly to forehead or displaying any betraying emotion.

*This is a critical step in your preparation for performance. You can **train** yourself to maintain a professional demeanor during a lapse. I have found a dramatic improvement in performance ability when students accept this fact, when they feel **committed to continue**, minimizing the interruption and remaining deep in the music.*

When practicing performance do not allow yourself the indulgence of any physical gesture of annoyance with yourself or any verbal explanation for a lapse. It is the music which is important, not how you feel about the slip.

*We feel a sense of responsibility to the composer to tell his story as well as we can, to the audience to communicate with continuity and consistency and caring, and to ourselves not to expect perfection—we are doing our best. If we feel an obligation to behave calmly, it helps us to feel calmer. **We know we have done our preparation homework with dedication and if a lapse should accidentally occur, it is acceptable, it is okay.***

*Let us reemphasize the fact that **errors are a part of life.** In all areas of our daily lives we make mistakes; it happens all the time. It is entirely human and to be expected. I don't think I have ever been to a concert where there were none. You need to believe this and not demand the impossible. Be fair to yourself.*

If, on the other hand, we are thoroughly prepared to handle lapses deftly, rather than dreading them and hoping for perfection, we will be realistic, more comfortable anticipating performance and most important, free to express the music.

Repeated training in this performance technique and attitude will make a distinct difference in your confidence level.

Children Learn to "Stay in the Story"

It helps young children to discuss staying in the story. "The audience is listening to the story you are telling and they want to know what happens next!" Older children will understand too that they are projecting a mood, an atmosphere, with their music almost as an actress does in playing a part in a drama and they should not break out of the role if they stumble. You sustain the mood you have created, even acting as though all is well, as you move smoothly and directly to your next familiar landmark.

Preserving the Mood

Adults also need to practice remaining within the mood of the music and resisting distractions, whether fearful thoughts in the mind or awareness of people or happenings in the room. This should be included as another technique to be rehearsed consistently in home practice performances but the building of a rich inner imagery on which to focus and a full relationship with the music during study are most important to this effort. This emotional connection plus one's serious occupation with interpreting the music as persuasively and authentically as possible will together create a meaningful experience that involves the whole person and gives substance to one's concentration.

Vulnerability and Competence

It is very important to believe that it is all right to make a mistake. It is what you do right that counts, not what you do wrong. Minor lapses do not subtract beauty from the whole work. Indeed, if you allow yourself this human fallibility, you will be more at peace and therefore less likely to experience tension-caused errors. One must dedicate much thoughtful attention to absorbing and digesting this belief.

Our vulnerability is the natural corollary of the human warmth that charges the music with life. We cannot equal the inhuman standards, the mechanical perfection of the recording studio but we are real, we are alive, we are spontaneous, we sing and give from the heart and we can learn how to be both human and competent in this challenging situation.

Calm, Professional Behavior

We will be reassuring to future audiences and to ourselves if we learn, quickly, calmly and professionally, to resume the musical narrative at the next starting point and continue as though nothing has happened. In fact, we can feel delighted that we have successfully managed to solve this natural problem. We are learning a necessary performance technique. It is additionally comforting to know that some listeners, (who have not studied the piece as intently as you have) will not even detect the slip.

Learning this skill is as important as learning to deliver the music effectively and persuasively.

I recommend a "practice sandwich" at this stage as a daily plan to assure thorough coverage of the whole system. Of course, more layers are possible.
   a) Through performance, using starting point strategy, if necessary;
      b) Work on individual sections and study starting points;
   a) Through performance, using starting point strategy, if necessary.

Rehearse Starting Point System with Gradually Larger Groups

After rehearsing this technique at the safest level for oneself, we try it many times for our tape recorder as our very first audience; then several times for a friend, spouse or other relative; then (also on a few different occasions) for a very small friendly group and we will feel our ease increasing; later for a somewhat larger informal group perhaps at your teacher's or friend's home; next several times out in the community perhaps at an institution where you truly deliver a gift—where your audience will be most grateful for the shared offering and where you may also experience the joyful satisfaction of music as a healing art and a bridge to peoples' most profound memories. Next we are ready for a larger, slightly more formal gathering, developing adaptability by performing and using the starting point system throughout this period as many times as possible and finally, in recital.

*The significant result of this process is the confidence it engenders. You **know** you can handle performance conditions because you have done so numerous times. The total ambience of a recital and the emotions it evokes become familiar and thereby demystified. One is more ready to respond with healthy vigor each subsequent time.*

All though this period, you are undoubtedly nourished also by the warm appreciation and encouragement you receive from people in your audiences. The sense that you have successfully communicated energy and conveyed beauty to other human beings brings a feeling of fulfillment you will treasure. This very valuable feedback adds to your growing confidence.

Support System Reassures Performer, Avoids Fear of Failing

*Another salient factor in the process is that once one has experienced in performance the reassuring security of this support system, **it will usually not be needed**. It is sometimes the fear of failing that makes one fail. Given deep and thorough preparation, accepting and even treasuring one's humanity, **believing that it is acceptable to err and knowing you have a rational method for managing errors**, the likelihood of a lapse falls dramatically.*

One's mind, freed from the business of worry, is released to focus on musical details. One's emotions are available to evoke the fullest expression of the composition. One's spirit is free to plumb the work's profundity and soar with its ascent. One's body is liberated from strain, able to enter wholly into the physical task of delivering the music with vigor.

Meaningful Patterns Unify and Simplify Memorizing Process

Most of us would not be intimidated by the call to memorize and perform a piece of four measures length for any audience, however auspicious. In a sense, what we have done is learn a logical sequence, a series, of four-measure pieces—no problem!

Similarly, most of us would be confounded by the challenge of memorizing a multidigited and lengthy figure, yet we have successfully and unconsciously committed to memory a large number of friends' seven and ten digited telephone numbers, each patterned into groups of comprehensible length and meaning. The principle is roughly the same. In the music, as in life, we have memorized by dividing a continuum into meaningful parts (Introductory thought, Theme I, Bridge, A major development of I, etc.), and effectively rejoined them with awareness of their structural logic and characteristics. We have also "practiced" the telephone numbers repeatedly and they carry many associations—imagistic and emotional—that connect us to them and enrich our learning process as well as our memory and retrieval of them.

Maintaining Continuity During a Lapse

Sometimes it is possible during a lapse to maintain continuity of sound and mood in some way that minimizes the interruption in the flow of music, while one searches briefly to reestablish firm ground or shift to the next starting point. (It should be emphasized that the period of time we are dealing with here is a very few seconds in length.) This is a valuable skill one might develop after having learned that the bedrock knowledge of starting points is totally reliable and available if one prefers simply to move immediately to the next one. Such continuity is preferable to a complete break, however short, and can be practiced frequently in the same indicated sequence of preparatory performances.

One might try sustaining the current harmony in some sort of arpeggiated holding pattern if it feels appropriate, hovering briefly in the flavor of the moment. Pianists may be able to continue in *tempo* with one hand, either a solo melody or an accompanying figure. One might improvise simply with a recent rhythm, hold the last pitch or chord a bit longer, repeat it for a while, or spin any threads one naturally intuits to match the mood of that instant.

A musician can use the safe haven of practice performances to work at leisure on this technique, viewing it as a refinement, a more advanced ability to be attempted after one has learned in performance the wonderful security of knowing and being comfortable with the starting point system. Its success, in fact, depends upon the confidence thus engendered as well as the depth of our immersion in the musical moment and commitment to preserving it.

Improvisation

It will help immeasurably if you feel competent creating spontaneous sound on your instrument. So we here launch a mini-lesson on improvisation. It is an absorbing activity which can become an important part of your life if you choose to develop it. Improvisation is much easier than you would think and quite attainable for everyone, especially those of us who already play an instrument or sing.

The joys of self-expression are certainly a major reward but one also attains an ease with music-making of one's own invention which is a great comfort when deprived of the printed page. When you forget what Schumann said next you don't feel utterly bereft. You are perfectly able to create a momentary sound pattern fairly appropriate to the piece if you have previously improvised in that tonality, texture and mood. It is somewhat like mending with the same colored thread as the fabric.

Once you have experienced a creative musical interaction with your instrument you don't feel alone when Mozart deserts you. You still have the clarinet in your hands and in your mouth. You feel comfortable with your long term companion. You two have been through much together and you know each other well. You also have a sense of the *tempo* of the piece, its pacing and momentum. You know, too, the next starting point as well as you know your name, precisely what pitch and key to resume. It is then as natural as could be to improvise an arpeggio or bit of scale which gracefully brings you to that point to rejoin your keyboard or string partners.

If you are playing solo flute or unaccompanied cello or violin, you have even more freedom to spin an alternative phrase that continues the flow up to the next thought, which you have practiced so many times that it is waiting for you—as familiar as your own front door.

Another considerable benefit is the opening of a window on the composer's process. You begin to see how the parts of music fit together to form a work of art. With this light cast on the process, it is clarified, seems possible for you too and might even lead to some composing. It does get the creative juices coursing. And after you have explored the harmonic life of a tonality with the given texture, it is so interesting to see what Beethoven did with it.

Obviously improvisation is a big subject and, in fact, I have a book on the back burner which more fully develops the possibilities and techniques within a highly personal framework. But just to give you a taste and a sense of your ability to become engaged with this delightful activity, I include a few starting ideas now.

Letting it Happen

If you have already done some improvising, this will seem most elementary and really, it is unnecessary for you. But for those of you who have never thought to try, it may be a revelation. Let's begin with piano, where the simplicity of ready-made pitches and keyboard ease our entry. This will also apply somewhat to harp, classical guitar and any keyboard instrument. In fact, much will be adaptable to any instrument.

Think of the key of a piece you are currently working on. Let's say it is in a minor and we'll just rest our hands comfortably and flexibly on a broken tonic chord in each hand, that is, A-C-E, and an octave higher another A-C-E. Feel a steady pulse and let a mood emerge, playing the keys from bottom to top, consecutively, then simultaneously, using damper pedal to blend the tones richly and establish an atmosphere that is warm and fluid. Once you feel comfortable with this texture, experiment with occasional longer tones on the same keys in the right hand—that is, rest on either A, C or E while the left hand continues to roll in the same rhythm and mood. You could repeat any note that feels right to you, perhaps responding to the desire to hear a pattern of either melody or rhythm. Anything you do is acceptable—this is your music.

Enjoy the sounds that emerge. Enter this experience with a contemplative cast of mind, open, ready to discover where your instincts will take you. Give this fledgling-you a chance without judging. The music will represent a kind of revery, a musing. Here is yet another opportunity to practice the letting go we know in performance—the liberation of your personal creativity, the letting-it-happen feeling rather than the making-it-happen feeling.

Just let your fingers lead you. They are familiar enough with the mechanics of your instrument and you have been absorbing the language of music all your life. Now your own message will be freed and begin to take flight.

When you feel ready, start in your right hand to include the intervening notes B and D. You might find a simple scale melody with a basic pattern—the simpler the better for two reasons: 1) consecutive melodic pitches are easier to control physically and, 2) they are immediately discernible as music whereas leaps are more challenging to handle logically. Your experiments will sound more musical if you don't strain for novelty. Begin with simplicity and let it develop in a very relaxed vein.

Why It Sounds Like Music

You may wonder how this can work harmonically. Is it really that easy? Why does it sound like music? The fact is that if you play a melodic A, C or E it will match your basic chord. If you play a B or D as a passing tone, that is, without dwelling upon it but immediately moving on to a chord tone, it will sound just fine—many musical compositions do just the same. If you do dwell on a B or D, either as a stressed sound or a sustained passing tone, the dissonance thus created will be resolved when the melody moves to the next note below or above— behaving somewhat like an *appoggiatura*, a nonharmonic tone on a strong beat which resolves downward or upward a half or whole step.

You will probably want to vary the harmony once you've established some flow. You could try the IV chord first—A-D-F as a refreshing change, then later, V—G#-B-E.

Your piece may come to a natural close but if you need to make it happen, a gradual *ritardando* will help effect a feeling of completion.

You may immediately pick up the knack of improvising, but if it feels a little strange to you, be persistent. Another day, another mood might be more successful. Let the broken chord tones flow again, interspersed with bits of the scale, or a different "starter." Remember to conjure up a particular mood, listen for beautiful tone and feel a steady pulse.

More Launching Pads

Clearly this is a conventional chord structure. It is a good way to begin if your ears are attuned to a traditional sound, or as a take-off point for more exotic destinations. The possibilities are infinite; one can vary the pattern, the texture, the harmony, the rhythm, register, *tempo,* volume, et al.

Here are some more launching pads: (where you travel is totally up to you— these are just ways to start the flow. Each of you will perceive them differently and that is how it should be.) Repeating intervals of all sorts as an accompaniment (experiment!), triads built on thirds or fourths, throbbing chords, a seventh chord as a melodic generator, syncopated melody against accompaniment, a short (two, three or four-note) motif as a foil for a slow-moving melody, slow overlapping tones, whole tone melodies with a whole tone *ostinato* pattern below, pentatonic scale tones used similarly (high register black keys with pedal instantly create an impressionistic sound quality).

The Importance of Dissonance

You may want to hold onto the dissonance at times, rendering the perceived conflict as the "meat and potatoes" rather than the spice of your musical language in a given moment.

A beginning adult student, who last year responded to an improvisation lesson with an immediacy and sensitivity that astounded me, came back in a week to express a radiant sense of discovery he had found in improvising. Describing how much he was savoring the experience he added "especially the dissonance." What a statement. There was a world of meaning in it which he has begun to appreciate.

This kindly person recently reminded me of my response at that time: "Yes, in *music* you can resolve the dissonance." I was very happy to know I had said this, because it seems to me not only true but it may perhaps pinpoint the meaning and power of music for human beings throughout the ages and across cultures. Biologists who seek to determine the survival value of this universal and persistent activity of *Homo sapiens* might examine the effects, both physiological and psychological, of this phenomenon. *In music one can experience and then resolve dissonance.* There is a felt alternation of tension and release within an emotionally and aesthetically satisfying context.

Of course, other art forms impart a feeling of tension and release but there is something about the total entry, the physiological, emotional, psychological and aesthetic identifying with music that can generate an especially potent and profound catharsis.

Winds, Strings and Singers

If you sing or play a wind or string instrument, you might try first a simple major or minor scale, slowly and expressively shaped with fine tone. You could vary the rhythm and see where that takes you. Try adding an arpeggiated pattern, ascending, descending, more bits of scale, a climbing, yearning sixth or seventh with some melodic follow-through. You will probably feel a desire to repeat melodic or rhythmic motives that arise in a most natural way. If you can find another musician who will listen sensitively to your wanderings and respond in a musical dialogue the resulting conversation will stimulate your own experiments and contribute to a more complex texture.

Adventure

Take this adventure wherever it leads you. The great joys of improvisation are its variety and its intimacy. It will always be different and it will always tell the story of who you are and how you feel in a given moment. Your state of mind will be reflected in your music directly, without words.

And your growing musical knowledge and technique will inspire ever more satisfying expression in your own music. It is a road you can travel forever.

To return to our original point, it is most helpful to know that you can improvise, that it *is* possible and that you have a ready, comfortable ability at your fingertips if you need it.

PROBING DEEPER

How I Feel During Performance and Practice

I have tried to describe how I feel during solo performance in an effort to better understand this phenomenal state and perhaps help others a little. At first I include performing-for-oneself in this category and later focus specifically on playing-for-others. I discovered that most features are the same whether I am performing for an audience or practice-performing at home, or even in earlier stages, starting to play the whole piece interpretively, putting it all together and going for continuity, going for "the music."

The distinction is very clear between these situations and that of the analytic, trial-and-error stage of learning, when we are crafting, repeating, stopping to correct, working by phrases and in sections.

There is also a gray area, as with many antitheses, where some of the activities overlap and I feel a combination of both states. I will describe that too.

Immersion and Surrender

The first thing that strikes me is the depth of immersion I feel, the totality of the immersion in the music. It is surely a "becoming" of the music, a one-to-one identity with the sound, momentum and mood. The music surges around me and charges through me. I feel I *am* the music, so wholly do I experience it. As pianist William Westney so aptly contributed in a discussion at the 1987 Denver Conference[1] "you don't know where you end and the music begins."

One expression that seems to sum it up is that I feel "plugged into an energy source that comes from the music." It directs me and keeps me riveted on the music. I can rely on this intense feeling of connectedness to inspire me and keep me on track. You might imagine yourself "plugged into" that bolt of energy to vitalize your connection to the music.

When I further attempt to define the very special state of mind I feel during this immersion it is elusive. If I ask myself "what am I thinking?" or "where is my attention focused?" my focus shifts to the training of attention itself and what I am thinking changes. The brain cannot examine itself.

But I *can* let myself feel this extraordinary state, enter it completely and wholeheartedly and then, immediately afterward, imagine it, conjure it up "recollected in tranquillity" as Wordsworth said.[2]

I recall then a vivid sense of surrender to the music, a letting go. I feel during performance a release of many controls one usually feels, a giving-up of oneself to the musical experience. There is also a surrender of most of one's awareness of peripheral events, of material objects in the environment, even of clock time—i.e., anything outside the musical tide.

---

[1] As stated in Chapter I, this conference was titled "Music and Child Development."
[2] Quotation to be found in the Preface to *Lyrical Ballads.*

Intensification of Senses and Spontaneity

At the same time, ironically, there is an extreme intensification of the senses of hearing and touch and "feeling"—that commanding but anatomically unlocatable sense. One is keenly sensitized to tonal quality, volume level, nuance of melody and rhythm, harmonic progressions, pacing, melodic intervals.

I feel myself to be highly vulnerable to the changing moods of the music, the unfolding drama, the characterization of ideas—all on a nonverbal level, a level of sound-symbols.

I do not feel bound to a preestablished interpretation. It will be largely similar to a carefully thought-out plan which has been evolving and thoroughly digested over months and years but I do not consciously adhere to it. I permit myself the freedom to alter it, the flexibility to respond as the person I am today, in this room, with this instrument, with my current relationship to the music, with this atmosphere, with my sense of this audience. In short, with spontaneity and sincerity and a live, moment-by-moment interaction with the music. I am *with* the music.

Vision

A few thoughts on vision; it is particularly interesting. Most of the time I feel I have a sensation of seeing the keys without specifically looking at them or ordering them. My actual gaze is trained on a special area that seems to hover above the keys. I feel I am rather looking at the music which fills up somehow the space between the keyboard and my eyes as well as surrounding both of us. This sense of the music's being there before me is almost palpable and I keep my concentration focused on this intense aura of sound.

I must be seeing the keys and my fingers plying them but the choreography of motion is so intrinsically part of the total kinesthetic response built up in practice that one seems to see without seeing—indeed, much music can be played with the eyes closed or totally without benefit of sight. The patterning in the neuromuscular system must be impressively and surely etched for such security to result.

In other words, I "see" the keys not as discrete objects, but as I feel them and participate with them in music-making, as melodic or rhythmic or harmonic partners, as tactile and expressive collaborators.

Profound Absorption

So this state is like a kind of trance, if you will—"a state of complete mental absorption." There is a suspension of time and place and some rational processes but at the same time the senses are very active, sharp, constantly at work, evaluating, altering, feeding back to muscles—all informed and unified by the intent of the music.

Activities that involve minute and subtle changes in pressure, weight, speed and use of limbs are ongoing, *unconsciously*, although they are wedded to and rooted in my *conscious* awareness of the music and my long evolving interpretation.

I know I am moving my fingers, touching keys, hearing sounds and responding with my foot on the damper pedal, hearing and responding in fact to a multitude of sound-experiences, but I am not making conscious decisions to do all these things from moment to moment. As neurologist Frank Wilson puts it (Jaret 1987), one "trusts the program" already set in place through hundreds of hours of careful work. We need to prepare with devotion in depth and breadth in order to feel safe to trust our program.

In his book, *Tone Deaf and All Thumbs?; An Invitation to Music-Making for Late Bloomers and Non-Prodigies* (Wilson 1986), Dr. Wilson describes the physiologic basis for these phenomena in "ballistic" muscle action which involves "advance programming."

> It is now recognized that highly skilled movements, particularly those that are rapidly executed and brief in duration, are under the guidance of a far more complex control system than is required for movements which can be corrected by ongoing adjustment, or so-called current control...details of the movement must have been completely worked out in advance, in a lengthy trial and error process, so that the movement can be executed when it is called for...in a nearly automatic way...
>
> —(pp. 49, 50)

He goes on to add that:

> Another equally significant feature [of ballistic control] is the striking change in muscle responsiveness that occurs in this condition. The physical fluidity which a performer enjoys when he or she is "on," or is playing "unconsciously," almost certainly stems from a marked shift in the physiologic behavior of muscles coming under a ballistic mode of control.
>
> The experienced musician may actively seek an inner state during performance in which the muscles feel warm, relaxed, and light, and use that feeling along with auditory information to confirm that things are going well...
>
> —(p. 51)

With an Audience

To continue my description of performance feelings, now before a live audience one must observe an additional, extraordinary state of alertness, a total mobilization of one's body forces, an acute marshaling of strength, ability, sensibility. One feels an extremely keen sense of involvement, of activity which may be complex and demanding in one sense but quite simple in another, since one's utter and complete concentration on the thread of musical meaning ("plugged into that energy") unifies and integrates all activity—all maneuvers, feedback cycles, mental and physical processing of information.

One feels total concentration, total alertness, total commitment to the music, physical readiness to move, emotional readiness to give oneself to the music and to the moment, to give one's energy through the music to the audience.

Comparison with Analytic Phase

To understand the different states of mind functioning during performance and during the earlier analytic, trial-and-error phase, we need to return to the role of the critical faculty—that essential evaluative voice.

When I am judging repetitions of a phrase, listening for ways to improve the sound, my critical sense is very active. It is consciously working, trained on fine details of the learning and refining processes. In this nitty-gritty stage, when we are involved with concrete elements, specific aspects of training, the critic is the overseer, the dominant voice in our proceedings. This is a more rational stage, although the emotional connection is always there, informing our decision making.

As necessary as the critical voice is to the analytic stage, the letting go, the openness to the music and entry into the emotional tide are vital to performance. *Both reason and feeling are always operating, but in different proportions at each stage.*

The rational processes are more unconscious during performance when the overwhelming drive is to communicate with the power of human emotion a whole work of art, rather than honing one's vision of it.

However, though the analytic voice is stilled in performance, it must be vitally at work on some level, deeply assimilated into our activities, or we couldn't function. The critical process at this stage involves aesthetic and motor decisions that are keyed into our inner programming. But they happen now because we *let* them happen rather than making them happen.

There must also be access to conscious reasoning powers as I have found them occasionally ready for on-the-spot decisions like…"well, that's interesting, the pedal doesn't seem to be working right—better omit the next piece…"

The Intermediary Ground

There is also that gray area I mentioned—the intermediary ground in the learning process, after the very basic work and before we are ready for through performance-practice.

As larger chunks are fluent and the level of interpretation entered, we need to make deeper and more prolonged contact with the essence of the music in order to help us sense flow, suspense and release, nuance, drive. We start to experience more of the surrender, more entry into the emotional current, though we are still crafting our translation. One can even feel this kind of release when repeating sections and phrases.

In fact, practicing is more enjoyable and productive at any stage when we maximize the amount of letting go compatible with learning and refining the music.

From my experience, we probably don't go as deeply into the unconscious processes as we do when performing, though we obviously enter the realm since much information has already been digested by our neuromuscular system. (See also "Letting Go and Control" below.)

Clues to Your Own Process

Perhaps you have picked up some clues in the foregoing discussion. Maybe your analytic voice has not been involved enough in the early stages. Or you have turned the reins over to your emotions too soon. Or perhaps you have not practiced letting go, that vulnerable sense of release, as a regular part of your preparation in gradually increasing amounts, so that you will feel comfortable and familiar with it in performance.

You may find that balancing these elements in more appropriate proportion during each phase will help you prepare better and enjoy performing more. Or you may want to dig a bit more deeply into the nature of your evaluative or critical side, especially if it nags you about your ability to perform, disparages your musicality or attacks you in general.

Dialogue with Your Critic

You may discover more confidence by finding the strength and wisdom within you to talk back to your internal critic, to have it out with him and take charge. Try the written dialogue technique described in the journal chapter or maybe a conversation on your tape recorder.

We need mental clarity to concentrate on our music. Confront any muddled thoughts or feelings; get them out on the table and try to analyze them. Our early influences and attitudes *were* powerful but we can deal with them creatively now from a new perspective.

What exactly does your judging self say? Can you recognize any destructive elements? You need to sort out this residue from the past and contend with any pressures exerted on you by others as well as those which are self-imposed—difficult to separate sometimes.

Find out more of what your critic has to say by talking things over with him, and in the natural give and take of these imaginary conversations between the voices which are both really parts of you, you will find the responses to his judgments—perhaps getting down to roots.

Think through what he is saying and find the constructive, positive alternative. There are always two (at least) ways of seeing things. You can become the winner in this debate through reasoning and persuasion. The answers will come from within you. A suggestion to launch you: "That's obsolete! That's the old view. Now it's like this. What is relevant today is..."

Now that you recognize the vital work of your critical voice, you might also let him know you need him, in the right role, at the right time, doing the important job of evaluating. The critic has an essential function as a reasonable, appropriate director. Accord him a place with appreciation, not with fear. Become friends: "I need you to help me listen sensitively, perceptively, to help me grow as a musician. Let's do this together."

Correct the nature of your "relationship" with your evaluator. You are in charge. You are a whole person, who loves music and needs both your reasoning and feeling selves to find satisfaction in music study and performance.

With harmful voices out of the way, you are freer to work on the constructive program we have brought forward. Have more dialogues if you need them—even every day if necessary. As your feelings evolve the issues may change and you will need to keep thinking positively and clearly. But you will also enjoy increasing ability to control the situation as you notice improvement and growing confidence in the other areas of preparation.

Practicing performing is very important. Here you work on intense concentration, training yourself not to allow negative thoughts to intrude.

At an appropriate stage of study you can also practice consciously directing your critic's perceptiveness *on the music, not on you.* Consider this another skill to work on and develop. Practice focusing it on a reasonable assessment of the sounds you hear. Keep it busy, listening, measuring, directing. Experience this often, with awareness, during practice sessions so that it becomes natural and familiar.

What we want to eliminate is the voice of the overwrought critic, not the constructive critic which is much needed to participate in the joy—indeed elation—of a well-prepared, communicative performance.

It will be easier to retire your critical voice to an unconscious, positive role in performance if you learn to connect vividly and identify wholly with the music. The inner world of imagination can be powerful and compelling—a realm you will enjoy inhabiting.

Journal work will help you tap into your artistic stream. And the dance we describe in Chapter VII will help you feel more emotional and physical freedom. Be aware as a piece is arriving at a stage when you may allow yourself to exercise more spontaneity.

You can frequently experience the sensation of release in the safe haven of your home, learning to deal with the consequences and developing your support system to back you up.

Indeed, this whole book is concerned with laying the foundation for you to know such security that you feel safe to let go.

Letting Go and Control

It may help to consider further what we are letting go *of.* I think it is, in part, some ordinary restraints and self-protective mechanisms which are useful in many situations. In performance however we need to feel free, spontaneous and expressive. Physical and emotional restraints which are usually advisable can be impediments to our freedom to embody the musical flow.

We are also letting go of "the rest of the world" in a sense, of everything outside the sphere of the music, in order to give ourselves wholly to it and forge a unity.

If these ideas give you the shivers perhaps you could explore the roots of this feeling in a dialogue with letting go.

Also, may I reassure you emphatically that I feel that I am still in control despite the surrender. One controls events *through* the music even as you give yourself up to it. As I play, I feel secure, not adrift at sea.

There is much to make me feel secure: I know I have done my homework. I know that I know the music in detail and structure. I know every starting point. I have rehearsed using them. I know I may make a mistake and I know that that is normal and okay. I feel secure that I know how to handle that situation.

I am familiar with this feeling of vulnerability when speaking from deep sources, when open to the music, when caring about its beauty and wanting to communicate that beauty to the audience. I do not mind feeling vulnerable.

I feel most intensely the giving aspect of this communication as I find the emotions within me to match the music.

I feel secure in the very depth, the rootedness of the experience.

It *is* a challenge. I enjoy the challenge now that I know how to prepare.

Attitude Toward Performance Can Evolve

It is encouraging to observe that one's attitude toward performance and one's relationship with an audience can evolve over time through progressive stages from tolerance of the excitement, to management of it, to pleasure in the act of communication. Performance does become easier the more you do it, given thorough and appropriate preparation.

A Protective Cocoon

In the earliest stages of our plan to enhance performance confidence, one can practice imagining (also in graduated performance situations as described) a protective cocoon woven about oneself, composed of the beauty of the music, one's communication with the composer and one's feelings about the music.

One learns to concentrate on the intense reality of the music-making, remaining within this encircling, gratifying and comforting sphere, separated from outside influences, not permitting any distracting messages to enter the cocoon and learning to brush them away instantly, whether they are inner naggings related to one's self-image or to previous performances or awareness of the audience in any way, its expectations or reactions. Thus one can learn to focus concentration on the music alone, within the warm safety of this imagined cocoon.

A next stage permits awareness of the audience's receptivity but retains the protective cocoon of the music. One enjoys projecting the essence of the music as a gift to the audience from the safe haven one has learned to create.

Finally, one actually relishes communication with the audience, secure in the knowledge of how to perform as well as study, aware of the uniqueness of one's personal contribution to music and to audiences—happy to share, hopefully to move. One begins to know the rare fulfillment of the act of performing music, in which fine art is recreated, given new life and offered with pleasure to one's fellow creatures—bridging the distance between us and healing the pain of the human condition.

I have seen many adults progress successfully through these stages—one, for example, who began with such severe anxiety that she could not even complete one phrase for me at our first meeting. Teachers need to understand and empathize with such feelings in both adults and youngsters who wish to perform, guiding them securely through all phases of their preparations.

To Reverse a History of Performance Anxiety

I would advise a musician or student who desires to reverse a history of performance anxiety and heal the wounds (or a beginning adult-performer) to observe the following *in addition to all other measures delineated throughout the book.*

Select for your turning-point experience a short, much-beloved and technically comfortable piece with a moderate *tempo* and study it so thoroughly that you could reproduce it on manuscript paper. Absorb, digest, linger over the harmonies until they are your friends; study the rhythm, melody and all other elements with similar appreciation, using the techniques I have described.

Intimately blend your specific knowledge of details with their real sound as you work. Achieve as well a physical grasp of the piece that leaves not a whit of doubt in your mind. Steep yourself daily in your new philosophy.

Use the preparatory moments of peace to contemplate, to rehearse repeatedly and to absorb in a meditative frame of mind any particular personal objectives you may have identified. These might include such matters as body ease with a supple, freely moving torso that allows an uninhibited flow of energy and emotion or easy, slow breathing for physical calm and comfort and as a model to allow the music to breathe too. Let yourself breathe and you will let the music breathe.

If you tend to begin at too rapid a *tempo*, use this moment to feel a deep sense of leisure and hear the beginning of your piece at the appropriate slower speed, letting it sing in your inner ear long enough for you to feel it in your bones.

Intense involvement in the music is the best antidote for self-consciousness. Develop a concern for making it as beautiful as you possibly can and emphasize this in your preparatory moments. Think daily of immersing yourself in your sound, diving deeply into the emotional flow and listening acutely for the kinds of effects you seek. Build a habit of devoting your feelings to this task and they won't flow toward concerns of self.

Prepare over a long period of time so that you have lived with the music, allowing it to ripen and mature interpretively, probing the deepest levels of meaning. "Overlearn" this short work until you are one with it, heeding emphatically all facets of the preparatory process, including personal and artistic enrichment. Observe particularly the starting point system and strategy.

Having once discovered that you *can* do it, play this piece for many informal and only later, somewhat more formal, audiences to build your confidence. Then you might gradually increase the length and difficulty and *tempo* of works to be performed in the future. Your new positive attitude toward self, music and audience will begin to erase the old and replace that mental baggage from the past.

Perform Only Well-Ripened Pieces

Furthermore, I recommend to all but the most accomplished and experienced performers who know their own abilities and limitations that you perform only pieces that are thoroughly committed to memory, well-digested and ripened and tried in many settings. Only later, when you are familiar with the performance process and your confidence is established, should you experiment with shorter preparation periods.

Anticipation and Control Reduce Stress

Laboratory experiments studying stress have resulted in findings that substantiate my work with performance. Two critical factors that alleviate the physical symptoms of stress are: 1) advance awareness of conditions and, 2) ability to control a situation.[1] The preparatory process thus far described acknowledges

---

[1] Studying the role of control in stressful situations, Jay Weiss and M.E.P. Seligman "placed three groups of rats in adjacent shock compartments. One...group was able to terminate the shocks by turning a small wheel. [A] second group had no control [over the shocks and a] third group...received [no] shocks." Later biopsies showed that the "non-shocked group was...normal [and] the greatest numbers of ulcers were found in the group" which had no control over the shocks.

both of these in that one knows that excitement will be there in performance (indeed, one has already learned to understand and channel it in carefully planned stages), and one knows further that one has a well-rehearsed strategy for dealing with it realistically and comfortably.

Practical Realities of Performance Situations

There are other practical realities of performance situations that can be anticipated and defused to enhance psychological readiness.

For pianists, who have the added challenge of performing on a variety of instruments, one should be familiar with the action of the piano, its timbre, capacity for nuance and pedal function. This is most important for inexperienced musicians or those who are trying to refresh their performing abilities. Unfamiliar sounds or mechanical difficulties in the midst of a well-practiced interpretation might distract a neophyte.

Similarly, for all of us, advance knowledge of stage arrangement, seating, piano position, lighting, acoustics and even room-temperature are useful. The most well-prepared technique can suffer from cold air, shivering arms and freezing fingers. The angle of the light on your finger board or music rack and, of course, sufficient lighting are basic needs which should be attended to prior to performance.

The physical components of differing architectural settings may affect your emotional responses as well as your carefully prepared details—volume levels and proportions, textures and pedaling decisions. An acoustically dry room might require more attention to tone production, resonance and projection. Another environment might even be inspiring, inviting your spirit to soar with your sound into the far reaches of a handsome, larger-than-accustomed space.

Simply seeing and feeling the setting helps too. In the beginning especially one should minimize environmental surprises and maximize familiarity in order to avoid shocks to one's system and to concentrate effectively on the music.

It should also be said that a musician achieves flexibility by learning to respond to the varied actions and sound-qualities of different instruments. It is, in fact, a requirement of pianistic training since we need to be ready to create beautiful sound on whatever instrument is provided. One's interpretation should not be fixed to the feel of the home keyboard. We learn to hear an ideal sound in the

---

"A second study...measured whether it is important to be able to predict or anticipate a stressful situation...One group...received no shocks...the other two...received shocks with equal frequency [but] in one [group]...the shock was announced via a warning buzzer. Weiss found that the group that was not forewarned...suffered the greater number of ulcers" (Restak 1984, 118).

inner ear and strive to discover the best ability of a given instrument to match that model. Developing this adaptability is a vital skill for a pianist. Play on as many different pianos as you can.

Moreover, one makes new discoveries even in worked-out pieces when an instrument with rich resonance in a particular register helps us to hear the music with a fresh perspective.

CHAPTER VI

YOUR BODY'S INNATE ABILITY—PHYSICAL PRINCIPLES

Thorough, complete and totally reliable physical control is essential to our constructive program of performance preparation leading to confidence and comfort. I would like to make this point emphatically without elaborating a technical method or style per se, a subject deserving of separate and highly detailed treatment, including demonstration. Technique is a huge and complex topic in itself, requiring lengthy discourse to do justice to it.

I speak of technique specifically as a pianist because I believe an authentic description of such skills must rest on a lifetime of hands-on knowledge. But it appears that the principles involved have relevance for all of us. Although many of the specific examples are pianistic, I think you will find the greater part of what follows applicable to your own work.

Having a sturdy sensation of support from your physical contact with your instrument, as well as that substantial support we have built in our bonding with the music and performance strategy, will stabilize our foundation for a secure stage presence.

There exists a great diversity of systems of technique and we have all heard compelling performances with differing physical approaches. General proficiency and the development of particular skills have been involved throughout the progressive stages of learning described thus far. Here we will merely reflect upon certain physical principles and concepts relevant to performance preparation.

Tactile Interwoven with other Learning Modes

There are many modes involved in learning a piece. Indeed, technique should not be perceived only in the sense of developing speed or strength or accuracy but in terms of acquiring the coordination and skills required for all aspects of a rich interpretation and *in service of the music*—sensitive touch, control of a broad spectrum of dynamics and timbres, fine balance, clear articulation.

Tactile learning is intimately interwoven with other forms—intellectual, visual, aural, imagistic and emotive—and security is best composed of a blend of the highest development of all of these. Muscle movement is trained, sculpted and evolved in union with the total kinesthetic activity of your body, the senses acting as a bridge between the inner world of mind and emotion, and the outer world of objects.

Unity and Spontaneity of Body Action

Indeed, it is enlightening to consider technique as a function of the remarkable unity and spontaneity of our body action, the senses constantly assembling information, our nervous system transmitting it, the brain sorting, registering, deciding in synchronicity with continuing sensual input—able to receive information from and send commands to our organs of touch, hearing, seeing.

In the act of performing, all of these activities are further informed, organized and shaped by your aesthetic faculty at a higher level of integration involving criteria of taste and knowledge, infused with the emotions and directed by the thrust of the music.

Freedom of Movement

These natural processes are best effected by a technique which is likewise natural, avoiding uncomfortable exertion which might lead to tension and pain. Flexibility in all joints and muscles throughout the body is essential and enhanced by a sense of buoyancy in the arms, shoulders and torso, with legs free to move and balance the torso as necessary. Indeed, speed and accuracy as well as the command of complex textures are directly related to *freedom of movement* as much as strength. The whole body needs to feel comfortable, alert, ready-to-go.

Awareness of Muscle State

Ease of movement can be an elusive quality for returning or beginning adult students and some youngsters as well. To achieve it one must first be *aware* of the current and changing state of one's muscles and joints, able to recognize and locate areas of tightness or flexibility in the whole body. Many of us store a tense residue of daily worries in our upper back, shoulder and neck muscles and some conscientious students will be seen to hold their heels up off the floor unconsciously as they toil to achieve a desired goal. We need to dissolve any constrictions or barriers to an easy flow of energy, get rid of any taut muscles.

"Your body already knows what to do," I sometimes say to a student. "You just need to *allow* it to play—to *let* your body dance and sing as it is meant to."

Swinging arms through full range of motion and all dancelike movements, especially to music and particularly to the piece under study, are helpful for releasing and warming up. Gentle stretching exercises are extremely beneficial as are easy torso twists, shoulder circling and head turns, *always being very careful not to force a movement beyond what feels comfortable. Be sensitive to your body limits, start easy,* do a little each day and you will find increasing flexibility and ease of movement as well as a heightened sense of well-being. (Check with your physician if you are unaccustomed to even such light exercise.)

I also advise such students to begin practice sessions by making a deep mental connection with the muscles, gently contracting (briefly) and releasing (for longer intervals) arm and hand muscles with arms hanging freely at the sides and eyes closed, concentrating on knowing exactly how each of the muscles and joints feel in each state, contracted and released.

We continue by allowing the arms with a sense of airy lightness and minimal effort, to *float* up to the keyboard retaining the released, buoyant, alert muscle condition, followed by very large, free forearm and wrist rotations and wave-like motions undulating through the hand with fingers gently resting on the keys. There should be no pushing, straining or tension—only a welcome freedom of movement.

During these movements and other basic exercises we continue to focus on how the muscles and joints of the torso, back, neck, shoulder, arm, hand and fingers feel, attempting to keep the flexibility and sense of release by mentally climbing into them and identifying intimately with their state. *Awareness* is the key here. Put yourself in touch with your body, the whole and each part. We are made so wonderfully—our system of joints and muscles permits an infinite variety of complex and graceful maneuvers. Enjoy your body's innate ability to move with natural ease and beauty.

This approach could be adapted easily to any instrument.

Transition to Repertoire

Another key element in these freeing exercises is a successful transition to the actual playing of your instrument. The awareness of warm, flexible, light muscles and free joints should be maintained throughout easy one or two note patterns, then three and more note patterns of gradually increasing complexity up to current repertoire level. When the emotional involvement of interpretation begins, it is critical that we do not equate intensity with tension.

Our eventual goal is to feel a oneness between a desired sound and the most comfortable, efficient motions required to make that sound—that is, an unconscious use of physique in music making. But if there are problems of tension one must go through a stage of very conscious work to achieve freedom.

Flexibility Must Precede Virtuosity

Because of the conditioning and civilizing (also inhibiting) effects of society, we sometimes need to be helped to feel free to move. When necessary I will say, always demonstrating the suppleness and the warm tone it creates, "let it be sloppy" or "almost sloppy"! This helps wonderfully, granting license to let go and injecting a welcome lightness of mood as well as muscle. It can easily be followed afterward by the necessary refinement of sound and focusing of touch.

Flexibility must precede virtuosity and is indeed so essential to it that one perseveres until it is achieved. A teacher should be diligent in observing, both in oneself and one's students, a freedom of movement throughout the entire body.

Imagery Helps the Release

Most students respond well to imagery, enabled to feel release by imagining arms as hammocks, wrists as rubber bands or bouncing rubber balls, airiness in the joints or spaces within the muscles. We even practice imagining a post-hottub feeling, where every cell in the body is totally at ease, released, entirely contented and free, learning to create this state quickly, periodically and before practice performances.

Sensitivity of Touch

Along with freely moving, buoyant arms, sensitivity of touch focused in the finger pads is quintessential. For technical security as well as fine, resonant tone production pianists need a warm, meaningful connection with the keys, finger pads alive and gently but surely gripping and *feeling* the keys, with a sense of being centered or balanced on the finger pad. One can, with flexibility and this responsive touch, shape and mold a rapid scale as effectively as a lingering *cantilena*, with the same warmth and intimacy one would use in modeling a handful of soft, pliant clay.

To understand how to draw beauty from an instrument with an ever-growing palette of tone, timbre, nuance involves a subtle set of skills which are infinitely rewarding to study and exhilarating to experience. The body speaks through the fingerpads. They are, in most music, the only point of contact pianists have with the instrument except for the pedals—a vital and most valuable resource.[1] The fingerpads must be keenly aware and expressive.

---

[1] We will not discuss the art of pedaling here except to point out the critical importance of keen listening and knowledge of appropriate style.

An Extension of Your Body

A performer must be aware too of his physical relationship *with* the instrument, in terms of attitude, posture, position as well as touch. The instrument, at best, will feel like the very extension of your body, more difficult to achieve for a pianist with our bulky instrument than say for a flautist whose light and wieldy flute can veritably float on the end of her breath or for the violinist or cellist, who surround their instruments, cradling them within their encircling arms. Later in this chapter we will develop the emotional and poetic character of this interactive relationship.

Interplay

It *is* a challenge to feel the piano as a continuation of oneself since one cannot lift, hold or carry it. Yet it is possible for a pianist to feel a confluence of grace and fluidity with the instrument despite its remoteness and size, that feeling that it is "out there" and not part of you.

One needs to experience not a holding back of body energy but a slight leaning into, a sense of giving to the instrument as well as to the music and the audience. Sitting on the front half of the bench will facilitate the feeling of a forward vector toward the instrument. One's energies flow through the music, through that essential fingerpad contact, *into* the keys and *into* the heart of the instrument. Indeed, the sensation of responsiveness from the keys' resilience, their bounding back into your fingers, creates a constant sense of giving and receiving, a true partnership.

Your whole body and your violin are vibrating together as the musical current charges between you; your sensitive response to its feel and sound determines your moves from instant to instant.

Indeed, you are actually playing *with* your instrument rather than playing upon the instrument. The keyboard or fingerboard feels like a friend with whom you are cooperating. Enjoy that give-and-take with it.

One must have also a sensation of "give" in the body, a torso free to respond to the lilt of the music, though not so much as to be distracting. We need total body flexibility and ease of movement as well as an effortless tone production to feel the ideal fluid interplay with our instruments. The piano will respond with a shining sound when technique is unforced, when the touch is sensitive and affectionate, providing a nourishing feedback one can feel and hear, completing the circle of relating.

This fluid rhythmic sense of acting with the instrument is not unlike the intuitive feel of good timing and movement as a tennis player strokes *into* a ball, his body swinging in a graceful dance with the racket and the ball, feeling one with the stroke. There is "music" in such movement and one hears the strings of the racket respond with appropriate resonance.

Body Position

One's exact position vis-a-vis the piano is very personal—we have all heard beautiful music produced from varied approaches. In particular the height of seating is variable as is the degree of torso tilt. A comfortable distance from the piano might be best described as not so close as to feel arm movement is crowded by the torso nor so distant as to feel one is stretching to reach the keys. The vital element is an easy interaction with the instrument with sufficient mechanical advantage over the keyboard and plenty of space to operate in.

Total Body Balance

The sensation of the entire body in balance is essential. Pianists need to feel a readiness in the torso to move horizontally as required by the ascent or descent of the music on the keyboard as well as the freedom to flow physically with inflections within tasteful limits.

Seated musicians will rest comfortably on the fulcrum provided by the buttocks with our legs free to position themselves in opposition to movements of the torso and also to absorb subtler shifts of body weight. The hip joints provide the pivoting action required by this overall body leverage and all the muscles and joints in the feet function smoothly to distribute our weight in a balanced manner, securely sensing the floor below.

Relating to your Instrument: Size, Shape, Nature

The size, shape and nature of your instrument, as well as your physical and emotional relationship with it, must play a vital role in music-making. It is a fascinating subject which I intend to explore in more depth and breadth another time, but I will here touch upon some of my current thinking. This byway truly represents an excursion into the domain of poetry. So be it. We musicians need to think about these things.

You may wonder why I say relationship *with* it rather than relationship to it since your instrument is an inanimate object. That is precisely the point—how animate or inanimate does it feel to you? I have enjoyed imagining such relating with a number of instruments, some of which I have played or collaborated with and others which I have known more indirectly—hearing, seeing, touching, discussing, thinking, reading about them from the perspective of their players. In addition, I have pretended, vividly, to play them in my mind, simulating the particular kinship I would feel with each.

Friendship

It may involve a subtle turn of mind, but I would encourage you to cultivate a friendship with your trumpet or your viola. It will help immeasurably in performance to feel a joint effort with your instrument, the two of you working in artistic collaboration to recreate the beauty and project the message of the music. You could not do it alone, (the singer being the apparent exception, although as we shall see, that sensation of solitude is fictitious; there are other supports for vocalists when they are perceived as such).

You need this ingeniously designed, sensitively calibrated and artfully wrought tone-producing creature to help you. You need to be friends. The oboe certainly could not do it without you either.

With all instruments too, there is the long saga of your times together through the years—your history. You have shared, hand in hand, some of life's most trying and most euphoric moments, building a union with distinctive attributes of its own. If I talk to my piano on occasion, I can imagine the ongoing dialogues that must take place between a musician and his double bass.

The more you grant a selfhood to your instrument, the more you will have the sense of a companion on the stage with you, sharing the responsibility and the joy of music-making. So there are really two of you—along, that is, with the music and the composer, two other central members of your cast. Now we're up to four! You see, there are scads of "you" up there and you thought you were alone. When you begin to sense the audience as individual and warm human beings just like yourself, you will discover that you enjoy their presence and feel *their* participation too.

I do not have any trouble imagining this instrumental persona. I realized when I read the poems of Gerard Manley Hopkins in college that his perception of "the suchness" of things struck a happy chord in my mind. It matched my own unconscious way of sensing the world of objects. I was delighted by Hopkins' poetry, one of the door-opening experiences that college is meant to provide.

Indeed, if we try to imagine a hierarchy of the relative liveness of inanimate objects, musical instruments must surely be near the top of the list. Their ability to talk, sing, moan, whisper, cry, when we understand how to grant them their say is astonishing. Each has its own magic built into the material—the carefully chosen and ripened wood or the purity of the silver or the precise alloy proportion—and how it is shaped and fitted as well as how it functions. We musicians need to take time to feel wonder at the very existence of our instruments—their redoubtable beauty, responsive nature and unique qualities of character.

Before we leave the subject of inanimate objects, I want to throw in another observation for your consideration and/or amusement. I have noticed that certain chairs, with the right lighting and at a propitious moment, will project great character and dignity—a selfhood that can be startling. From hand wrought chairs I see occasionally, I notice that sculptors are very aware of this extra "capacity" of chairs to embody a personhood.

If you have any doubts about the amicability of your friendship with your instrument, this might be a fruitful topic to pursue in your journal. Try an imaginary dialogue between you and him/her. It might be revealing and it could provide a clue to understanding and refreshing your feelings about performance.

Piano

We have already somewhat explored the piano keyboard as a friend. The sense of cooperating with it is dramatically enhanced when a pianist discovers the liberating effect of a springy interplay with the key action. We can imagine the keybed as a trampoline that bounces the finger, hand, wrist, and arm back up into the air, most readily felt in a staccato. Using the wrist and elbow joints as shock absorbers one can enjoy the same swinging interaction with the key with sustained sounds as well.

Feeling an ease of descent with the help of gravity and this resilience to help us ascend, the remaining work is slight. We can then experience an easy sense of play in the space above the keys, freed from the need many students feel to keep weight pressing into the key after a sound is produced.

The life analogy is clear: as with a friend when effort is unforced, when we are sensitive to the nature and responding mechanism of the piano, our relationship has an intimacy and ease. We indeed act as one to realize the music together. It is a joy to experience the instrument in this way.

Voice: You Are the Instrument

Singing is perhaps the closest to dancing. Your body is your instrument—performance involves only you, the composer, the music and the audience. There is no intermediary, no object, between you and them but, as we have suggested, there is great support to be discovered in your relationship with each of them. Since your body *is* your instrument, the dance work we shall describe is especially important for you. It will help you feel at home in your body, comfortable in the space around you and with other people.

Your very breath, the substance most intrinsic to life, is what you play upon to create timbre, melody, inflection. Your breath is you. Wind players too share this common reliance on breath. Thus your health—physical and emotional—is intimately involved in musical expression. There is a greater challenge and a greater opportunity, as well, in the direct expressivity you experience in song.

The nuances of our inmost being are revealed in our voices. It is very difficult to suppress the truth of one's real feelings, to banish it from the voice. All of the preparatory phases are vital for the singer to establish mental and emotional clarity. The techniques and interpretation must be so deeply felt and practiced that you feel safe to let go, to give yourself completely in the moment of performance to fulfilling the essence of the song. A thorough preparation leaves you free to speak the truth of the music, totally, wholeheartedly. You want to enter the music profoundly, to identify with the mood and message of each piece you sing, to merge with it, to become the music.

The feeling of giving to your audience is thus very personal and direct. You can reach out intimately, caringly to your listeners. You look at them, they at you. You engage them more spontaneously and actively in the experience of music making, in the emotions you discover in the music and recreate in the moment. By projecting the excitement powerfully and involving them intensely, you forge a close alliance with the audience.

There is a strength to be derived from this bond. If you are open to your listeners and communicate with them in this way, they will actually support you. You will not feel alone. The audience becomes a roomful of friends you speak to and care about, who need to hear your message, feel your spirit and be restored.

Strings

For all the rest of us, those remarkable objects called instruments are our partners in joint communication with the audience, except of course in ensemble works where we have even more colleagues.

String players embrace their instruments in a way that particularly suggests a human relating. The larger forms must feel especially like another person—cello, double bass, guitar, harp. Certain large winds also conjure up this sense of human apposition, intertwining with you in a manner all their own: tuba, French horn. You are always duetting, never alone. There is a feeling of comfort in this constant empathic contact, like a good conversation with a friend or a warm hug. Indeed, the entire spectrum of emotions possible in human relating might be felt with such an instrument.

The cello might be experienced as a beautiful other, a pliant and warmly articulate creature who can say for you in sound what you could not verbalize, whose tone plumbs the depth of unimaginable utterance, who rewards your appropriate touch with resonance.

The artful application of bow to string has so much potential; the myriad ways of setting the string to vibrate, the subtlety of pressures and their timing, the placement, the strokes, the collaboration with the left hand—the understanding of this response mechanism suggests all the complexity, frustration and reward inherent in human bonding.

Cradling your violin close to your face must surely affect your relationship with it. Both intimacy and intensity are kindled by the proximity. At times your parental instincts must be aroused by the fact that it is small enough to be held and carried about easily. One is moved to care for it and protect it. But I have also felt fierceness in a series of *ff* double-stops or driving thirty-second notes. Indeed, the potential heat must be magnified exponentially by the challenge of rousing a vast yet true sound from this minute being. Knowing precisely what kind of touch, pressure, timing, continuity or discontinuity will produce the sought effect, and doing it, must mark a Himalayan peak of human experience.

Winds

The wind instruments introduce a unique aspect of confluence with their human counterparts. In addition to the touch of fingers, a most sensitive part of the body in terms of nerve-endings, we feel the mouthpiece of our flute or trumpet on our lips, an even more delicate body part. The tongue, still more vulnerable, is also involved in the mechanics of tone production, subtly altering timbre, pitch and coloration. How intimate a joining with one's instrument.

Like the vocalist, you give your very breath in music making, but with an object, a collaborator you hold in your hands and can move with. This adds the element of dancing with and breathing with a partner, another person. Have you ever seen Richard Stolzman in concert with his clarinet or Rampal with his flute?

Your trombone or bassoon is a veritable extension of you, a continuation and alteration of your breath as it courses through its full length, tempered by accurate arm slides and sensitive finger touch, emerging as vibrant sound. And like the singer, you are acutely aware of body health, of lung power, as an essential element in your musical alliance.

As with the strings, the fact that you can hold and carry about the smaller winds may promote a tender, care giving quality in your relating (though most emphatically not exclusively) whereas the larger winds are more likely to suggest a marriage of equals.

Efficiency

A basic and undeniable physical principle is getting the most beautiful sound with the least possible effort. No matter what particular school of technique one espouses, this concept should be applicable. One aims for comfort, searching for the easiest way to get from point A to point B and make fine music while so doing. Efficiency in movement makes sense and is clearly present in successful technique.

Inventive Solutions for Knotty Passages

Imagination too is critical in solving knotty technical problems, as one choreographs the "steps" or movements to match the unique demands of the particular situation—tilting the hand just so, shifting the center of gravity slightly, timing a lateral arm glide, locating the most effective balance point, employing more or less finger, wrist or arm or even shoulder and back, adapting the fingering to suit the size and shape of hand and fingers (technical solutions often involve improving the fingering), visually targeting the goal note in a challenging leap, inventing a mental regrouping of notes that happily facilitates execution. Indeed, one also discovers that some so-called technical problems even dissolve in the light of a new *musical* perception, a different way of thinking it or hearing or feeling it.

Technique Depends on the Ear

Ultimately, technique must reside in the ear and will only be as good as the sensitivity and precision of one's hearing. To sparkle, a scale must be perfectly equal and one needs to be able to hear that equality of tone and duration to achieve it, modeling the ideal in one's inner ear, then listening to discern exactly where inequalities occur in order to erase them. We need to have an aural image of the sounds we want—a perfect *legato*, the tensile strength of melodic sixteenth notes, the degree of dryness we want in the *staccato* chords. Then we hear our actual sound, adjusting and correcting it as necessary. Indeed, our physical parts will cooperate best when informed and organized by a clear mental image, "conducted" as are the instruments. of an orchestra by a coherent musical intention.

Indisputably, independence and strength of fingers are fundamental requirements—operating best within that naturally coordinated, free movement we have described. While we all agree on the need for this basic competence the ways of achieving it are highly variable and personal.

Generally believed, too, is the virtue of warming-up before performance as well as selecting pieces appropriate to one's technical level. The latter can be critical to comfort and therefore confidence. One can with study feel secure if a piece is manageable but our whole preparation process can be sabotaged by an overly ambitious selection. A sensible plan aspires to a high standard of quality with pieces you can handle while working diligently at the same time to build your technique. It also enhances performance confidence to attain in practice a *tempo* well beyond the requirements of the music so that one has a good margin of security, never straining in performance at the very limit of one's development.

Solving Passage Problems

Also generally appreciated is the wisdom of concentrating special work on passages that seem to elude control (although certain exceptional artists might not require this particular effort, nor many of the other learning techniques that are so helpful to most of us). These passages should be isolated and practiced meticulously until they are as smooth as any passage of the piece, perhaps even the smoothest—with the cautionary warning to place them back into context after the extensive treatment. It is not enough to conquer the trouble spot without rehearsing the approaching passages. Gradually include more and more of the preceding and following measures, repeating until the freshly learned moves are naturally absorbed into the fabric. We may then, in performance, launch into them with musical vigor, secure in the knowledge that we have transcended the purely physical obstacles.

Understand the Precise Nature of the Challenge

The methods of attacking difficult passages are myriad. One must first, however, analyze and understand the precise nature of the particular physical challenge, determining the most efficient and aesthetically effective choreography of motion. Ask yourself, "why is it difficult for me—how can I move more comfortably?" The results of even the best practicing methods depend directly on the basic technique employed. They cannot magically transmute dross into gold. Indeed, poor movements so practiced will only produce more deeply ingrained and habitual awkward movements.

Never go into performance uncertain of such a passage; if you do, it is likely to be a vulnerable point, destabilizing mood and concentration. For psychological readiness, work until you feel solid physical control and *know* that you have it. Then enter the music completely and stay deeply involved with its sound and intent as you approach and complete the passage.

It is important not to hesitate as you come to such a passage but to drive on with full expectation of success, maintaining the depth of emotional commitment which permits such spontaneity. For. this insight and many other gems, I am grateful to Robert Martin, cellist and philosopher, with whom I have performed with the greatest pleasure.

Many Methods

Having solved our kinesthetic problems, we have many possible methods of consolidating these passages.

Working with gradual increments of speed on the metronome is a time-honored approach which works, especially if each speed is repeated until extremely comfortable before advancing to the next. With each tiny increase the fingers hardly perceive a change yet the goal *tempo* is eventually achieved. We should emphasize the value within this particular approach of the slower and moderate speeds, achieving accuracy and control by practicing precisely, solidly, with fine tone and flexibility, with every detail of interpretation correct. The sounds are more easily discerned, the patterns mentally absorbed and the muscle movements clearly set at slower *tempi*.

Russian pianist Isabelle Vengerova's "accents" in my experience have proven to be an extremely effective technique, rhythmically grouping twos (first down-up, then up-down), threes, fours, sixes, eights, twelves, sixteens (each grouping used if it corresponds to the rhythmic structure of the passage) and finally no accents, gradually increasing speed in each grouping and striving for a very close *legato,* muscle ease and resonant tone. It works like magic!

I have also heard pianists enthusiastically advocate the effectiveness of rapid practice of very short bits which are then combined, the theory being that the muscles learn their eventual roles by working closer to final *tempi,* simplified and digested by attempting only tiny portions of the material.

Similarly, many teachers advocate altering rhythms in the many possible combinations of long and short, the body system "resting" on the long and achieving ease with the increasingly rapid movements from short to long.

One can also train the muscles with mental grouping and regrouping of notes. This serves the dual purpose of experimenting until a preferred interpretation of directional goals and sub-goals is found as well as enhancing muscular versatility by sending subtly varying messages to the muscles.

Transposition of the intricate section will similarly increase adaptability. This is especially helpful with embellishments, which one can move diatonically or chromatically up or down.

Other approaches include playing the knotty bit both forward and backward, continuously. This sometimes helps to pinpoint the crucial move and sets the kinesthetic pattern comfortably in terms of where one is going as well as where one has been. A well-articulated finger staccato is also useful for pianists in developing incisive clarity and precision.

Body Wellness Affects Self-Image

It seems appropriate to include in a discussion of physical preparation the wisdom of treating one's whole body with care, maintaining an overall health scheme with sensible eating habits and a good balance of rest and exercise, including varied movement and stretching. When working toward a full recital program, living with the special demands of touring or competitions, one might well imagine oneself in training in the athletic sense.

An awareness of physical well-being unquestionably affects our mental self-image, our sense of ableness, and the reverse is also true, as we have discussed. We need a general feeling of ready vigor, fitness, flexible strength and elasticity to perform at peak ability—physical energy equal to the spiritual.

When the performance time draws near, one should take special care to rest both oneself and the music, getting a good sleep the night before and not overdoing the day of the performance, either with exercise or practicing. Both you and the music will be fresher.

A final perspective on the subject of technique is suggested by this penetrating comment from *The Varieties of Religious Experiences* by William James ([1902] 1985, 170):

> ...a musician may suddenly reach a point at which pleasure in the technique of the art entirely falls away, and in some moment of inspiration he becomes the instrument through which music flows.

CHAPTER VII

BECOME THE MUSIC—AN INVITATION TO DANCE

We hinted at the full potential of dance for performers with the idea of bouncing a rhythm around the room to better appreciate its vitality and particular nature. And we mentioned the benefits of dance-like movement and exercise in achieving flexibility and freedom of motion in the torso. Now I would like to take you beyond that—to offer that dance itself, and a particular very personal kind of dance experience, can be most fruitful for musicians (and any of us). Undoubtedly, part of the benefit is simply the mental refreshment that any satisfying and coordinating physical activity brings. But there is more.

We feel a profound internalization of the music, a merging with it that leads to more sensitive interpretation. We experience a rare kind of emotional catharsis and an enhanced sense of physical ease with ourselves, our instruments, other people, audiences. And we grow more in touch with our own artistic impulses.

I like the idea of seeking this liberation through an aesthetic activity that involves music itself—the very substance that we love and respond to and seek a more intimate bond with. To find at the same time a greater understanding of our medium and a release of our inhibitions is a double benefit. There is a rightness and relevance in getting closer to music, which we need for performance, while we become freer physically and emotionally, which we also need for performance.

This is an invitation to dance.

Body Oneness with the Music

When you listen deeply and move to music, an emotional and physical bonding occurs, a sense of body oneness with the music. You absorb and assimilate the sound, letting it flow to your very center and permeate throughout your body. You feel the harmonies, the rhythms, the melodies chanting and surging in this center, *directing your body movements from within—not from the periphery*. This is a fine antidote (or better, preventative) for an undue focus on the mechanics of playing one's instrument, an over-engagement with the actions of fingers, hands, lips, mouth, arms.

One can immediately see that such identity with the music is the very condition that informs the muscles in fine playing. This kind of dance is, indeed, music-making with the whole body. It is also story-telling with one's whole body, as we shall see.

It functions not according to a detailed, preordained or rehearsed set of movements prescribed from without but inspired by a spontaneous inner direction only. Movements will be designed by a compelling whole sense of the music's drama. One feels the urgency in every cell of the body. An organic fusion seems to occur—music becoming the lifeblood itself. Through digesting and moving naturally with the music, we *become* the music.

Interpretation Enhanced

Returning to one's instrument after probing the inmost areas of personal response to music, one discovers a sensitization has taken place. Our ability to interpret the score before us is enhanced. If we continue to dance in this integrated manner as the days pass, exploring many different kinds of music with varied moods and ways of moving, we will begin to feel a more vivid, ongoing connectedness with music, both in practice and performance.

We will have learned to embody the music, to know the fulness of each phrase.

Emotional Catharsis

We also experience an emotional catharsis which increasingly frees us of "baggage" we may have been carrying about in our bodies for years. Frank Wilson, in a discussion of rhythm, speaks pertinently and poetically of muscle-memories of a "former dance;" that perhaps music can "suggest earlier movement histories which hold meaning for us" (Wilson 1986, 140). Through dance, we travel the vast range of music's metaphoric breadth; we touch the depth of its penetration of the human experience, its mythic knowing. Listening recently to the strains of Beethoven's *String Quartet Op. 132* in live performance, I heard this empathy so potently expressed in the music—"Beethoven understands," I thought.

But we are also telling our story as we dance; that is why we feel such an extraordinary release. Movement has symbolic meaning as does music—one is interpreting now with the whole body. Reaching high may express yearning; a shift of arm position and the reaching becomes celebration. Hands cover the face—one may be reliving a moment of pain. A tilt of the head—contemplation; a different tilt—defiance.

Endless numbers of more abstract and unnameable equivalents must be occurring as we move. *The music touches these wells of feeling, stirs them, permits us to know them aesthetically, express them physically, recognize them wordlessly, satisfy them.*

It is a process kin to that of simply listening to music or playing it on one's instrument or singing, but it goes deeper and is more basic. One is not concerned with adherence to a score or a complex set of physical maneuvers or involved with a meticulous and subtle feedback cycle of careful sound production and listening followed by precise alterations in those sounds. *One is free to personify the essence of the music, to bring to it unconsciously your own private mythology, to "meet with" the music.* Through body movements as natural to human beings as strolling or running or rocking a baby or beckoning to a friend or drawing a heavy rope over the shoulder, you "build yourself"[1] into the story of the music, interacting with the composer's offering at the deepest levels of human expression.

We experience an expanding and liberating spectrum of emotions, from those which are resonant with darkness—fear, anxiety, anger to compassionate feelings—empathy, benevolence, gratitude, love. Each kind of music, each composer, each piece and mood will touch different aspects of our persona if we allow ourselves to be kneaded and shaped by the music even as our movements give bodily shape to it.

Greater Physical Ease

You begin to notice a qualitative change in your physical and emotional sense of self in the world—a greater ease. You will also feel more comfortable with your instrument and, most appropriate to our discussion, with other people—an audience, for example; newly aware of them as "human beings like me," with all the needs and foibles and qualities and quirks of the human condition. This is especially true if one has been dancing in a group, as we shall see.

How does it work? My own personal experience may elucidate the process for you.

Gertrude Knight—"Your Own Way of Moving"

A comment by Patricia Shehan at the Music and Child Development Conference in Denver the summer of 1987 sparked a new connection and led me to consider the role of dance in shaping my own development as a musician and performer. Ms. Shehan emphasized the importance of large muscle movement in a child's musical education; (one might also leave out the word "musical" in that

---

[1]   Joel Krosnick, cellist with the Julliard Quartet, used this wonderful expression during a Piatagorsky Seminar at USC while exhorting a student to respond personally to his piece and interpret, to have a plan. "You need to build yourself into the music!"

statement but that is another large and fascinating subject). Of course, I thought, and why not for adults as well, remembering a significant turning point in my own life.

During a period of about ten years, at times bearing the beginning of new life within me, I experienced the kind of dance improvisation described above with a gentle and gifted teacher in Palo Alto, California—Gertrude Knight. There were many evenings when I thought I was too fatigued even to climb into the car (after a day chockfull of the caring for four little children, practicing, teaching *et al.*) but I was invariably energized and restored by the end of the session, filled with new inspiration and optimism.

A small group of us, varying in size from time to time, would step, stamp, swirl, swing and glide to a wonderful variety of musical forms and styles—all selected carefully to evoke and release a vivid personal response—from Beethoven Quartets to Beatles, African Masses to Greek, Israeli and Russian folk songs.

It is Gertrude's gift to help each person discover his own way of moving to music, through imagery and suggestions that invite one, ever so gently, to move— *but only when it feels right, only when the music calls you.* We felt assured that there was no single mysterious way beyond our ken but only our own vital responses to the music, our spirits consonant with it. She helped us to feel the music speaking through each of us as unique individuals, with corresponding ways of dancing as natural to each as our style of walking. We discovered as we danced that we were communicating at the deepest unselfconscious level. We felt keenly alive and sentient.

At class one evening when my family and I were about to move away, far beyond a commute to Gertrude's class, I tried to communicate my appreciation of her and my sense of impending loss. In that conversation she said to me, "You could do it, too," and a seed was planted which lay dormant for many years.

I have begun to realize how significant were those hours of dance in enriching my musical awareness, helping me feel comfortable with myself, with the piano, with other people and with audiences. Now my students are experiencing something similar and I want to suggest that you try too.

A Pivotal Evening

I will describe how you could begin but first I want to tell you about one pivotal and revelatory evening of dance, perhaps twenty-five years in the past, but as fresh today as it was then.

The music was modern—very disturbing, turbulent, raw, a large orchestral score. I felt myself entering the mood of this dark, compelling maelstrom of sound more completely than I had ever known before—pulled down into its undeniable, unrelenting vortex, expanding with the force of its churning, seething energy.

I could feel my body stretching into new shapes, my legs carrying me at an exhilarating pace, my arms reaching for the understanding I somehow sensed beyond the black clouds of dissonance. My spirit agonized along with the music, both of us searching to experience and to know.

At the end of the first movement I was nothing more than a crumpled heap on the floor, thoroughly devastated, limp...I couldn't move...

Then an amazing thing happened.

The second movement of the work began—slow, luminous, like the dawn of a new day. The fresh hopeful harmonies and warm melodies poured into me and, very gradually, I sensed a small stirring of renewed life at a very deep, subconscious level. I remained still, outwardly, but within a transformation was beginning to take place. It was like a new me was slowly forming as the peaceful music surrounded me, soothing sounds entering, occupying the spaces cleared by the raging storm. I began to feel more and more comforted, hope sprouting into a sweet sureness, a new selfhood.

And then, just as inexorably as I had been driven to join that feverish battle, I was slowly drawn to my feet once more—but now with a deeper calm than I had ever known in my life. I moved serenely among the other dancers as though I had never seen them before—feeling acutely the essential goodness, beauty and uniqueness of each person. I felt so fresh and pink that I was able to see that same purity in others, so comfortable with the humanity of this new self that I could greet each person—young and old, man or woman—as a friend, as a fellow being on this shared journey through life.

Having braved and survived the storm, I was reborn seaworthy—ready for the rest of my life. I felt strong and kindly—a new birthright permitting me to spin around throughout the group, filling the spaces between people, weaving them together with threads of caring, whereas I had previously circled only at the periphery or in the dimmer corners of the large room.

I was brimming with good feeling for other human souls. They did not seem separate or foreign to my own being anymore and I felt open to that essential humanness of each—knowing now that we were all of one fabric.

The euphoria of that remarkable transformation lasted for some weeks but its deeper effect has been permanent. I found it necessary to temper my openness with realism in the ensuing weeks but the sense of appreciation of other people and comfort with them, with myself, with my piano too (as I discovered later), and generally in the world, was distinctly enhanced to this day.

Getting Started

If you have done any kind of active large muscle movement or athletics, whether swimming, running, tennis, aerobics, brisk walking, gymnastics or any form of dance, it may be quite easy for you to glide into this experience. If you have been relatively shy about dancing or vigorous exercise, it may feel strange or awkward at first. But if you will persist and open yourself to the sublime and earthly powers of music to move you through space, a real treasure awaits you.

If you have been fairly inactive physically it would be a good idea to check with your physician before beginning.

A Warm-Up Experiment

Here is a delightful and easy warm-up experiment to help you feel the music in your very center. Find a few moments for yourself, wear some comfortable clothes, enter your living room and turn on the radio. The key in this experience is *letting* the music work its magic on you, not seeking or causing movement, but simply listening, feeling and allowing things to happen. Let yourself enter another realm. An artist is "willing...to permit unconscious processes of play to gain sway" (Gardner, 1982, 102).

Standing with your eyes closed, allow whatever music is in the air to waft about you; let the sound fill you up completely; let your body sway like a young tree in the breeze of the sound waves—only moving because you cannot help but move, your trunk freely rocking with the rhythm, your soul absorbing the mood of the music. At first your arms could hug your torso. Then, if they are moved to swing about like the soft green branches of the young tree, let them. If your body feels an urge to follow the direction of your arms—walking or gliding or skipping or prancing—let it do whatever feels natural. If you want to stop and sway again, fine.

Follow Only Deepest Impulses

Never force a movement. Listen only to your body's deepest impulses—those urges which are in tune with your inner sense of the music. You do not *have to* move anywhere. Simply enjoy the music throughout your whole body. Feel it pulsing in its own way in your center. If you only stand and sway as the music deeply enters your consciousness, it is enough—an authentic, complete experience. Anything you *make* yourself do, for any reason, is an intellectual decision, a conscious one tangential to our goal here which is oneness with the music—a deeply felt merging with the very marrow of the music.

Moods

Of course, the nature of the music you happen to find on the dial (or digit) might not lend itself to swaying. It might rather be frisky and become a tiny bouncing ball deep within you, impelling you to spring up and down a little—perhaps a lot. And then the bouncing might travel through your arms, jumping into your hands which might then flop raggedly about like a stuffed cotton doll, bits of music hopping off the ends of your fingers and into the room to join in the merry-making.

Or the mood might be sultry, Gershwinesque, talking to your shoulders until each side of your body was conversing in turn with the rhythm in the air. It might be celebratory and immediately light up your eyes and send your arms flinging skyward, pulling the rest of you into a swirling festival of motion. The music might be pastoral and gently lead you to stroll with pointed toe; it could be meditative, calling you to sit and rock almost imperceptibly on the wooden floor.

Stay with this first musical selection only as long as it has meaning for you—no longer; do not insist on a continuing responsiveness. The music may not be your cup of tea or it may hold your interest only for a limited time. It might not match your energy level of the moment or your mood or the time of day. If you feel a resistance to it, that is good. It is a sign that you are really allowing yourself to be vulnerable to the music. The rejection is as valid as affinity would be.

Flip the dial (or press the button) to another kind of music. Here is where the wonder of this experiment begins. Now let yourself open up to a new mood, a new rhythm, *tempo*, momentum, color, emotional range, energy level. Take the new music to your center and let it move you as it will. If you like it, continue. If not, wave your magic wand again and your radio will respond with something different.

After doing this for awhile, you may discover a more tender sensitivity to the varied items on your musical menu—some absolutely delighting you and others even repelling you; some speaking immediately in a voice you understand and others almost irrelevant. You become much more aware of your "gut" response to music. Your aesthetic antennae grow keener and you feel more certain of your tastes. Consciousness becomes more vivid, susceptibility more acute.

Within the spectrum of those you enjoy, you may find a surprising variety. You may also begin to notice pleasure in the anticipation of a fresh opportunity to know another mood—an eagerness to perceive another part of yourself in the next offering. It becomes a celebration of life—of all the human possibilities that are inherent in the composers' gifts to us, as relayed and enriched by the performers' humanity and received by us. This experiment helps you to understand yourself better, to *be* yourself better.

Intensifies Perception

I find it interesting that I am willing and even delighted to dance to some music that I wouldn't choose to sit and listen to. This music is somehow more meaningful to me as a generator of expressive movement. I will sometimes appreciate such music more even when sitting still, as soon as I feel and understand it to be music I would love to dance to. A shift in receiving mode occurs and I imagine myself moving to it, mentally entering the story. What does this mean?

This kind of music is apt to be dramatic, with vivid changes of texture, dynamics, gesture, timbre—strong contrast and colorful orchestration, often a large ensemble with operatic use of instruments. It is pictorial and suggests a program although not necessarily in nineteenth century style. The suggestion of a theatrical, adventurous narrative may be conducive to telling one's own story through movement. The waves of sound stimulate large body movement—running, swirling, reaching high—and create extremes of tension and release. Subtler shades of emotion are exemplified in chamber music, my usual preference, which deals with essences in an understated way and permits my ears and mind to participate more fully.[1]

I find that music I prefer is also enhanced for me when I am currently involved with dance, which intensifies my capacity to perceive all music.

Different Receiving Centers

You may observe another interesting phenomenon. I discover when I dip into the full range of the musical spectrum, including all portions of the culture, that different categories of music seem to talk to different centers in me. I can feel the shift from one kind of receiver to another as soon as I hear a new strain. It is dramatic and revealing. I am reluctant to define it too precisely, and you may respond with your own personal imagery that will be quite different. I will offer though, as example, that most classical music (the genre not the historical period) seems to speak to a higher physiological realm of being within me whereas certain forms of popular music—notably rock—is more visceral in its appeal. That sounds almost like a truism but its interesting aspect lies in the subtler shades

---

[1] I recently heard Itzhak Perlman describe his preference for chamber music in a radio interview. He spoke of the "purity" and "economy" of Beethoven's quartets, "so transparent because of the instrumentation...like a synopsis of his symphonic work." He relished "...the pauses, the spaces, quiet spots, the parts you *don't* play..."

of center-shift I feel between, for instance, folk song and popular ballad or from classical to jazz. I think a further catharsis can stem from exercising a variety of these centers: the vestige of the primitive in us as well as the refined, the earthy folk spirit, the romantic innocent, the sophisticated blend of heart and head in jazz.

A Serene Approach

I would like to describe now another way you might begin to move to music. It may be a more effective first avenue for you than the radio experiment or it could simply be viewed as one of many ways you pursue. This approach can effect a profound regeneration of the spirit—there seemed to be a time for it during each of Gertrude's sessions.

Select a record, tape or disc of particular serenity and depth of mood—almost any slow movement from a baroque or classical concerto will do. The effect of a solo instrument like flute or violin or cello seems to me to be an important element in the power of this technique as well as the interplay between the solo instrument and the orchestra. Apt here, perhaps, is the traditional analogue that hears the solitary melody of one instrument as the individual voice of mankind wending his way through, sometimes against, the world of the orchestra with all the rich potential for concord or conflict inherent in that metaphor. We seem so naturally to identify with the sound of that yearning bassoon as we move through the air; or with the wise cello or contemplative flute or probing violin.

Obviously many works offer similarly rich tapestries for weaving this introspective mood. Some of my favorites are the slow movements of Bach's *Violin Concerto in E*, Vivaldi's *Seasons*, Mozart's *Piano Concertos K. 271* and *K. 488* and his *Sinfonia Concertante K. 364*.

Lie down on the rug and *rest*, allowing the abundant tranquillity of the music to enter you and fill you. Breathe it in deeply and absorb it. With each breath let the comforting sound more and more into your lungs and throughout your body. Relax totally as the music gradually merges with you and nourishes you. Let every muscle contract and release, one by one, from feet to head, sinking with your full body weight deep into the floor as you exhale. Soon each cell will be vibrant with sound and you will feel one with the "energy field" of the music.

You may fall asleep. That would be fine, for the sleep would be a special one in which the subliminal power of the music would undoubtedly be felt. Try again when you are less tired or perhaps your awakening will find you deeply refreshed and ready to move, closer to the unconscious forces that shape our dreams.

If you do not fall asleep, you may begin to feel a need to move with the music as it kindles a warmth within you. As I described earlier, *only move if and when* you feel a true call impelling you from within. There is no prescribed way to move—we will each be different. There is only the generous spirit of the music to quicken yours and there is your intrinsic human need to express your feelings through movement as people have ever since life began. Even if you have never danced before, it will feel comfortable when you experience this deep identity with the music.

Let it happen *very slowly*. Stay in touch with your oneness with the music. That will be your only source of energy and your only guide to movement. Let the music speak through you.

At first your arms may want to wave slowly through the air, conducting the music. Or one arm alone might take up the thread of the solo instrument and weave it in and out, followed in time by your torso, as you sit up wishing to express the searching melody with more of you. You might remain seated through the whole piece, rendering the developing drama with arms and torso as fully as one may—sensing the tensions and releases with varied sweeps and surges of motion.

Or you may feel the music urging you to rise to your feet and follow the lead of your arms through space—standing and conducting or rocking, swaying, beginning to walk, spin, run or skip.

Even if you remain on the floor at rest, absorbing the music more deeply than ever before, you have had a most valuable experience. It will probably stay with you as a warm and beautiful memory. You will feel revitalized, at the least, by this new sensation of music at your very center and you will subconsciously associate music with that pervasive peace you knew as you lay there resting. You may feel an afterglow at your next practice session or a heightened sensitivity the next time you listen to music.

This enhanced oneness with music and calm relating to it will undoubtedly grow with each attempt to awaken your readiness to dance. Another time, or with another "starter," you will feel ready.

Remember that what the music gave you is what you give your audience when you perform—that revitalization.

Once you get launched you will enjoy exploring the abundant varieties of music—each mood and each turn of thought animating you in a multitude of ways. The prospect for self-discovery is infinite as you feel the sympathetic vibrations of each chord within you, each harmonic progression, each nuance and leap of melody, each change of pace, key, meter, color, timbre, composer, era.

Other Starters Stem from Imagery

Your adventures in dance will take wing from many kinds of images as myriad as music itself. We mentioned the sense of a bouncing ball in your center that might spring from a lively texture and *tempo,* gradually expanding through your torso and limbs as the energy grows undeniably within you, finally bursting forth from your hands and feet in sprightly fashion.

Another musical impetus might induce waves of arm motion as vast as the rhythms of the sea until the swells of sound send you whirling and waltzing about the room. A festive, jaunty character might launch you on an idyllic flower-sprinkling skip into summer. A regal *adagio* might inspire a courtly processional with a bit of pomp and ceremony, while a light-hearted *scherzo* might incite a playful child-like romp. The latter is usually a rare, welcome experience for adults and so refreshing. Refinding the ability to play in the context of serious, focused, grown-up life is an unexpected treasure.

Some of Gertrude's evocative images follow. Usually after a more energetic segment we would be resting on the floor and hear the silvery sound of a single flute. She would gently suggest that we spin the slender silver thread of sound around and we would begin with one hand to weave it in and out through the air, forming a shining fabric of our own dreams and memories. Spinning the silky flute melody was one of my favored images. It always sang to my spirit and led me into a luminous sequence that floated lightly in some inner space of the mind.

Sometimes we would be invited to let sparks of music fly from the tips of our fingers and we would fling scintillating sparks across the room to each other. Soon the spaces around us were alive with light and color and we all were fused together in the glow. This kind of fantasy is infectious. It opens human beings to each other and releases them freely into the dancing fireworks around them. It dissolves the spaces between people into whimsy and in the delight we feel, we perceive the delight of the other. What a unifying human experience. It is comparable to the warmth of unrestrained laughter among friends. You can understand how this sense of empathy will begin to color your feelings about an audience—fellow human beings who delight in receiving your musical offering to them.

Returning to being a king or queen, one might imagine a very tall crown on one's head, with the well-balanced carriage necessary to strut in appropriate splendor. Gertrude would suggest that our necks could elongate grandly and soon one's whole body was stretching tall and reaching to the ceiling as we paraded with the stately music. This vertical alignment of the torso has a freeing effect on one's arms which then would begin to gesture royally in classic fashion.

I am not a dancer by profession but I have had enough formal training to observe that the erect vertical axis with support from the abdomen and the lower back is essential to balance in a professional dancer (and, incidentally, it feels wonderful). It functions as a kind of plumb line around which movements rotate. The instrumentalist or vocalist needs that same sense of physical alignment. The idea of the ball of musical energy bouncing in one's center is also an ideal in dance—that authentic movement emanates from the center and one must feel it beginning there. For authentic musical interpretation as well the impulse must be felt in the very core of being.

We would sometimes swing imaginary ropes of music about or heave them across the room to another dancer. Someone might fancifully use their giant strand to lasso another and draw them in. Still more ropes of sound would be tossed until the room was webbed with them and we struggled to move among them—the entanglement a potent image of the darker side of the human search. Pressing against imaginary bonds that resist one's efforts can result in powerful dance forms as well as satisfy deep psychological urges. Soon we will get into the aesthetics of this kind of experience as well as the role of the psyche.

On other occasions, a musical texture might suggest fibers of gossamer lightness rather than weighty ropes and we would delicately wend our ways through a fine webbing of silvery strands, begun perhaps by that original flute and spun into a filmy fabric as our paths wove together. Imagine now the airy arm movements that would result from exploring the soft, misty spaces between dancers.

The Spaces Among People

The theme of dealing with the spaces among people is here sounded again. The heavy ropes would bind the dancers together in a mutual hardship whereas earlier the sparks had lit up a celebratory aura which we freely entered and shared. Now the fine filaments suggest a soft impressionistic blurring of the boundaries between individuals. This issue of how one interacts with the space around one is important for us as performers. The freedom one feels to penetrate this area is closely related to one's sense of personal freedom, self-expression and comfort with oneself as well as one's attitude toward others and a more general sense of safety in the world. Is there fear and uncertainty or caring and security? This condition must surely affect the nature of one's relating to one's instrument and the spirit with which one greets an audience.

Once one had moved through that space among the others when it was lighted by imagined fireworks or webbed with resisting ropes it became possible to enter that same, now familiar space more easily another time, with another music, in another mood, or in a social context, a performing context.

After a shared experience barriers were melted. One felt not a hard-edged quality about other human beings but a flow of spirit among us—a "we're all in this together" feeling. The development of this freedom to move out into that space, to soften your own edges, can make a significant difference in your attitude toward performance—a great leap forward. The giving to the audience depends on this capacity to get outside yourself. It is related to the ability to go beyond yourself when you are submerged in the beauty of the music, to give to it as you merge with it.

Whatever experiences you may have had with people in the past, now you can begin to feel a commonality with all people. In basic ways we're all the same. We have similar hungers, thirsts, dreams, fears, hopes, worries. Composers too share in this humanity. Through their art, they talk to us, try to tell us what they know of these things, how they feel about life. Their art reaches out to us and says we're in this together. Here is a part of me to show I mean it. Your audience shares the humanity as well—all of us are together as you convey the composer's message along with your energy and caring.

Spatial Compositions

One began to enjoy sensing the overall design created by the moving dancers—underscoring it by threading a line with one's own path among them. The composition would keep changing as others continued on their own course and this shifting pattern through space and time formed by our bodies in juxtaposition with each other became a very satisfying artistic event. I found the awareness of this design, formed as I moved among the others, an almost palpable entity and felt great pleasure in it.

We became sensitive to the complementary shapes formed by two people in motion to the music. Occasionally mirror images would result if dancers were so moved or a contrapuntal theme would be struck in the group as pairs would imitate or greet each other in passing. Graceful scenes would flower. We enjoyed viewing them as much as creating them. The human body, spontaneously responding to music, can be a wondrous instrument.

In retrospect I increasingly appreciate the genuine artistry that flourished on those evenings. At the time I knew it was an important experience for me, a unique one and a deeply satisfying one. But with the insights of more living and thinking and studying I now understand why.

Gertrude Knight's Dance Improvisation Class

Aesthetic and Psychological Rewards

What happened was rewarding both aesthetically and psychologically. Without entering the arcane realm of defining art, which I will leave to others who are committed to examining that perennially elusive subject, I can say that the artistic components of the experience were compelling for each dancer both as an expression of personal aesthetic intent and in terms of participation in the larger design—a sensitive appreciation of the whole vision.

Moving to match the music was a creative act—sound-forms stimulating the human body to respond with three-dimensional kinesthetic forms through space and time. (That adds up to five dimensions, doesn't it?) The nature of one's aesthetic was responsible for invoking the particular way one moved; movement was unique, unrepeatable, genuine and wedded to a moment shared in time with the music and the other dancers. The subtlety of the groups' interweaving of shapes into an overall design was a further expression of the undeniable art involved.

The fact that such movement stems from a dancer's deepest emotional urges adds to the relevance of the experience. In shaping moves that reflect the currents of our sub-conscious lives as they are stirred by sound, we are creating a complex art form. One might almost say an ultimate art form since these spatial compositions are symbolic of our very life journeys, our psychological selves.

Such dance is thus a deeply integrated and integrating creative act—a marriage of sensitivity to music with the natural impulse to move rhythmically, fueled by one's own psychological imagery. Such dance is the shaping in space of one's own song.

It is interesting to ask, as artists, whether this important form of human expression requires a viewer or critic and certain criteria of beauty to anoint it as art? Let's think about this.

Intent and Perception

Subjective factors must surely play a large role in an artistic event, both in producing and receiving or participating. In my experience, I have found that the intent of the originator and the perceptive mode of the receiver are germane.

Working with young children in piano improvisation with the goal of producing a musical result, I discovered that two important elements were feeling an organizing pulse and creating a persuasive beginning, middle and end. But an even more vital factor was *the intent to make beautiful sound.* One evokes the aesthetic impulse simply by the intention to do so, by attitude, thereby conjuring up the muse and tapping into a rich source of invention. I use imagery to help these youngsters release the flow of their creative juices, to lead them into the appropriate frame of mind, a technique I develop in my book on improvisation.

Some years ago I had an arresting art gallery experience which exemplifies the consequence of the frame of mind of the receiver as well.

The exhibit was billed as Environmental Art and I entered the gallery on the UCSD campus with antennae attuned to aesthetic reception. One work I encountered on my slow stroll around the room was a simple black box from which a solitary voice emanated. The speaker was engaged in a long litany of extinct and threatened species of animal life on the planet. I stood silently listening to the lengthy report, overwhelmed by the power of the presentation. Because of the particular vulnerability I felt in the presence of art this work had a powerful impact on me—an indelibly etched impression. The artist was Newton Harrison and it was his first large ecological work (1969).

Therapy and Art

I remember someone saying, when I described those dance evenings years ago, "That's therapy, not art." Yes, it certainly is restorative, satisfying, therapeutic *and*, to me, it seems it is art as well. Anyone who has been seriously engaged in artistic pursuits such as writing or painting or composing will attest to such a feeling of refreshment after a good session. Artists often describe their motivation to work in terms of need—even sometimes as a driving, merciless master. Doing their art is curative; could they survive without it? I believe art and therapy are not mutually exclusive. They go hand in hand.

One feels healthy after dance improvisation—clear-headed, fresh, energetic, catalyzed, ready-for-life, also somewhat released from the inhibitions and the burdensome weight of obligations many adults feel in our civilization. One can then welcome responsibility with such a feeling of fulfillment.

I am reminded of the fascinating work of Manfred Clynes described in his book *Sentics* (Clynes 1977). After participating in an experiment designed to study the shapes of curves resulting from people imagining a series of emotions and pressing a button rigged up to a graphing device, the subjects said they felt refreshed. Clynes concluded that even such a vicarious experience of a variety of feelings had a therapeutic effect on people. But this was only an interesting and unexpected side-effect. A series of studies carried out among different cultures revealed that the graph curves formed in response to specified emotions such as love, anger and fear were similar. It is tantalizing to speculate about dance-shapes evoked by such emotions. Clynes also studied graphic shapes formed by musicians' responding to the characteristic beat of several composers.

FURTHER THOUGHTS ON PERFORMANCE PREPARATION

Avoid Last Minute Changes

A void last minute changes in interpretation and especially in fingering. They may stick but probably will not. More important, the conscious effort to remember this new element might shatter our long-nourished and carefully wrought kinesthetic response—that synthesis of mind, body and spirit in finely-tuned balance.

Innovations and Variants

Experienced musicians with well-established patterns use their judgment and experiment from time to time with innovations, perhaps short-cuts, in preparation plans. There are, too, the rare naturals for whom performance is a simpler event, who will respond well to challenges such as lack of time, new music freshly learned, risky technique, etc. After you have used the thorough approach successfully and you are feeling confident and aware of your powers as a performer, you may begin to experiment with variants as you see fit.

Reviewing Known Piece for Performance

When preparing a known piece for performance the same process of analysis and memorization is necessary and profitable, all the areas to be explored thoroughly with some modifications.

We begin to study the work in sections as we would a new piece, with the same interest in the details of composition, the recomposing process, but we soon feel the excitement of discovering deeper levels of understanding. Although we are reanalyzing and rememorizing, we begin to experience that wonderful feeling of encountering an old friend with fresh perspective; new beauties emerge bathed in new light. In a sense the music gives more to us because we now have more to bring to it—it reveals greater depth of thematic relating, rhythmic connections, harmonic bonds and echoes.

I recently had this experience with Brahms' *Intermezzo in b flat minor, Opus 117 No.2*, as I found a diminished c chord behaving as antithesis both to the b flat minor chord in Theme 1 and to the D flat major chord in Theme 2, albeit clothed in an A flat dominant 7th. I had not noticed this particular structural resonance in past journeys with the piece and I felt closer to the inner core of the music through this revelation as well as more anchored in the harmonic realities, the harmonic facts of Brahms' discourse.

Intermezzo in b flat minor, Opus 117/2 Bars 1-2

Intermezzo in b flat minor, Opus 117/2 Bars 22-24

We may think we knew a piece earlier but we invariably find not only new facts but new emotional depth when we explore again. The closer we get to the degree of maturity, experience and insight of the composer, the more we are able to enter his imaginary realm, to plumb his profundity, to realize his intention.

There might be a tendency in reworking repertoire to depend overly on the emotional connection, which is so familiar, so strong and so comfortable. For secure performance, however, even of this old friend, we still need solid, thorough grounding in detail, omitting none of the preparatory steps. The sequence of study may be altered, however, as we continue immediately with each phrase from the fact-finding stage to the interpretive, reworking the entire piece in this manner, phrase by phrase, rather than remaining at the basic learning level throughout the piece and later traversing it again to work on interpretation. The coloring stage comes sooner because there is already a strong foundation in detail. But invariably with each revisit our ideas will be richer and our emotional response more intense.

We continue to refine and polish, many times examining sections and the whole, consolidating and penetrating even deeper. An experienced performer will require less exposure to trial performances, but *some* are still desirable. One needs to know and evaluate one's own ability and security.

Conducive Environment

It is helpful to have a quiet, private place in which to work, a responsive instrument and the respect of housemates, their tolerance of the sounds of music in the progress stages. Sometimes careful scheduling and compromise are necessary.

Teachers and Confident Performance

Many of these suggestions can be passed along to students by a nonperforming teacher. But the whole process is most effective when a teacher is hopefully en route or has experienced first-hand the joy of confident performance, *believes* it possible and can reassure all students with positive and convincing energy.

CONCLUSION

INTEGRATION

Cultivate Rich Inner Life—Enjoy Giving

To respond energetically to the challenging outer world of music, to our demanding, rewarding and evocative instruments, to the literature, to the waiting audience, a performer needs to cultivate a rich inner life and a healthy philosophy in addition to studying systematically. Teachers, as well as parents, have the opportunity and the responsibility to establish fine values early and provide young people with a life-long foundation for self-esteem, a deep love of music and comfort in performance. They can personally impart confidence, leading students gently to their own self-discovery.

The emphasis must be, not on displaying, but on giving. To play the music with joy, one needs to want to give, to exult in giving, to give with love.

Value your Uniqueness

We also need to believe we have something to say, to believe in *what* we have to say as well as how we decide to say it. Value your uniqueness—no one else can be "you" as well as you can. Each person, unique in his own particular combination of inputs and attributes, brings together all his life experiences in service of the music.

Sense of Wholeness Enhances Concentration

There is much compartmentalization and fragmentation in our world today, many pulls on our energies. The act of performing demands focus, concentration and serenity even as music itself is an integrating force. When we have doubts, our minds are split and our energies diffused. We need to prepare for performance by living our lives wisely, nourishing a complete self, developing personal depth and emotional wholeness, cultivating a healthy philosophical framework for the act of performance, enjoying broader learning and intellectual growth as much as we thoughtfully and carefully build sureness into our performing system and sustain the essential and energizing love of music.

We need to study the music in depth and connect with it at all levels, from the smallest detail to the overall message. We need to feel an intensity of emotional engagement to endow our interpretation with life and insure its integrity. We need to develop technical dexterity that will transcend the physical barriers to a full expression of the composer's intent. We need to provide ourselves with the psychological security of a reliable support system in performance.

Just as the creative artist will, after accumulating ideas, allow unconscious forces to act upon them, reaching into the deepest sources, synthesizing emotional, intellectual, psychological, aesthetic energies to finally ignite and transform the material into a whole work of art, the performing artist, to distill the essence of the work, needs also to synthesize the information and all levels of the self into the recreative act by operating at the highest level of his integrative forces. This fusion, this letting go, this soaring can only occur with the assurance of solid grounding in the facts.

Develop all Parts to Initiate Constructive Cycle

Even our discussion of performance preparation has required artificial divisions for the sake of clarity. In reality, we know all parts and processes interact and affect each other. Indeed it is only the mind itself which creates the categories—cognitive, physical, psychological, aesthetic. All relate and function within our prodigious nervous system. This can be a wondrous system capable of sublime joy when all parts are cooperating in an integrated manner, initiating a constructive cycle of satisfaction and offering a personal gift to society, a unique human view. But a destructive cycle can ensue from the lack of stability in one part, irritating another part and starting a downward spiral.

The Mind—Central Processor

It all begins with the mind, central processor of all body activity—calculator, creator, predictor, storer, recaller. Our memories—reservoir of past experiences of music, of performance, of oneself in the world, one's relations with family, friends, teachers—all feed into the currents of the present activity, informing and shaping one's response to the challenge of the moment. Thus, our picture of performance preparation has been painted on the broadest panorama, over a long period of time, probing deeply, calling upon wide resources.

I hope fervently that future performers will benefit from enlightened teaching and thorough, thoughtful preparation. And I believe with equal fervor that musicians who are already formed and feel some degree of insecurity in performance can reeducate themselves to a healthier attitude.

> We are all afraid of many things; we probably can't help that. What we can try to do is not give in to our fears, but face them down instead. There is excitement in that.
>
> (Holt 1978, 171)

You will never discover how good you can be until you accept this challenge.

Plans for Now and Future

By now you probably have discovered areas in which you would like to work to improve your skills as musician and performer and enjoy more learning. It might be helpful, if you have not already done so, to find your journal and write up a current evaluation of where you stand as well as a coherent plan for development.

You could describe your feelings about music, about yourself as a musician, about your instrument, perhaps about a coming recital, a particular piece or composer. Whatever comes to mind is relevant.

It might be stimulating to imagine also how you would like to feel and where you would like to be musically.

You might list and prioritize any points you would like to develop and then set some goals to structure your growth—both near and future goals. Some samples, depending on your own personal needs, might be:

1. Study in depth and memorize eight measures of a given piece this week;
2. Study starting points of a known piece and rehearse performance strategy to prepare for next month's concert;
3. Organize daily practice procedures;
4. Today do some deep listening to a tape of my sonata, with my eyes closed, and let it move me to dance if it feels natural;
5. Spend some time daily working on relaxed technique and fluency, a different key each day;
6. Have a dialogue with my critic at least once a week until we understand each other;
7. Go to library this summer and explore music shelves;
8. Subscribe to annual concert series this fall;
9. Buy a journal tomorrow and write whenever I feel moved;
10. Finish studies in Piston's *Harmony* this year;
11. Play for family once a week and friends often;
12. Learn one short piece thoroughly, at leisure, and perform when it's ready;
13. Prepare with depth and breadth and *give* that solo recital next spring;
14. Organize a performance group of like-minded friends for informal recitals, dance improvisation (rotate being leader and choosing tapes) and discussions of shared concerns, interests, and ideas;
15. Gather a group of professional colleagues to do same (and throw out the pills!);
16. Take the violin out of the closet tonight and make friends again.

Obviously these samples might be very different from the goals you project for yourself. After you decide on your goals, you might prioritize and organize them. Devise a first plan with a reasonable trajectory. Satisfy yourself that you *can* improve by succeeding with this modest plan. Then make another plan. Keep trying, keep growing. If you are not pleased with any particular result, learn from the experience and keep going!

We all need to keep remembering that we are constantly in a state of becoming, that we can change ourselves, that *we are what we do*, that our daily choices shape us, that we can grow and improve in whatever direction we choose.

Persistence

A few words on persistence and determination from John Holt who took up the cello in mid-life. He describes in *Never Too Late* an initial euphoric feeling of "surprised delight" that he could play along with other musicians in a small chamber orchestra although in later evenings "the sharpness of those feelings wore off."

> But that was all right. I didn't feel any let down. I had learned, and know even better now, that those ecstatic messages that tell us that we are doing what we love and need and ought to do, don't come everyday. If we expect and insist on that much 'reinforcement' *every* time we do something, we will never do anything. Those messages come only once in a while. We must learn to trust them. Having been shown the road, we have to stay on it, at least for awhile, even if it is sometimes a little hard.
>
> (Holt 1978, 158)

Integration

Recalling the Toffler quotation (page 50) on modern man's penchant for dissection, let us reemphasize the need for integration. The human being himself is the ultimate synthesizing body. By all means, analyze the parts, study intimate details, work on sections for control, absorb pertinent information with delight, but what puts it all together persuasively and gives with love to an audience is a whole, healthy human being with a fine sense of self-worth, whose attitude toward the act of performance is sound, who feels reverence for the music and knows great joy in giving it new life.

REFERENCE LIST

Bernstein, L. 1962. *Young Peoples' Concerts for Listening and Reading.* New York: Simon and Schuster, Inc. © The Leonard Bernstein Foundation, Inc.

Briggs, D.C. 1975. *Your Child's Self-Esteem.* New York: Dolphin Books.

Buber, M. [1947] 1955. *Between Man and Man.* Boston: Beacon Press (first published in England 1947).

Clynes, M. 1977. *Sentics: The Touch of Emotions.* New York: Anchor/Doubleday.

Dorian, F. 1942. *The History of Music in Performance.* New York: W.W. Norton.

Gardner, H. 1982. *Art, Mind and Brain.* New York: Basic Books, Inc.

Gombrowicz, W. 1988. From the cauldron of literature: An exile's journal. *New York Times Book Review,* March 13.

Green, B. and Gallwey, W.T. 1986. *The Inner Game of Music.* New York: Anchor Press/Doubleday.

Harrell, L. 1988. *Los Angeles Times,* June 11. Originally in *Ovation Magazine,* May 1988.

Havas, K. 1973. *Stage Fright, Its Causes and Cures, With Special Reference to Violin Playing.* London: Bosworth.

Hofmann, J. 1976. *Piano Playing, With Piano Questions Answered.* New York: Dover.

Hollander, L. 1988. The price of stress in education. In: *The Biology of Music Making,* ed. F.L. Roehmann and F.R. Wilson, 47-51. St. Louis: MMB Music, Inc.

Holt, J. 1978. *Never Too Late; My Musical Life Story.* New York: Delacorte Press/Seymour Lawrence. (reprinted 1991 by Addison Wesley/A Merloyd Lawrence Book, Reading, MA.)

James, W. [1902] 1985. *Varieties of Religious Experiences.* (In *The Works of William James.* Cambridge, MA: Harvard University Press.)

Jaret, P. 1987. Why practice makes perfect. *Hippocrates* 1(4):91.

Kahn, A.E. 1970. *Joys and Sorrows—Reflections by Pablo Casals.* New York: Simon & Schuster, Inc.

Kirsch, R. 1976. *Los Angeles Times,* June 29.

Kottler, D.B. 1988. David. *Radcliffe Quarterly.* March Issue.

Levertov, D. 1973. *The Poet in the World.* New York: New Directions Publishing Corporation.

Nyberg, D. 1971. *Tough and Tender Learning.* Palo Alto, CA: National Press Books.

Pater, W. 1898. *The School of Giorgione.* Portland, OR: T.B. Mosher.

Restak, R. 1984. *The Brain.* New York: Bantam Books.

Reubart, D. 1985. *Anxiety and Musical Performance; On Playing the Piano from Memory.* New York: DaCapo Press.

Ristad, E. 1982. *A Soprano on Her Head, Right-side up reflections on life and other performances.* Moab, UT: Real People Press.

Sacks, O. 1984. *A Leg to Stand On.* New York: Summit Books, a division of Simon & Schuster, Inc.

Schneiderman, B. 1983. You, your child and music. *Journal of the Suzuki Association of the Americas* 11(4): 23-32.

Strunk, O. 1965. *Source Readings in Music History, Vol. 1. Antiquity and Middle Ages,* selected and annotated by Oliver Strunk. New York: Norton and Co.

Suzuki, S. [1969] 1983. *Nurtured by Love.* New York: Exposition Press, 1969. Athens, OH: A Senzay Publications/Ability Development, 1983.

Toffler, A. 1984. Foreword: Science and change. In: *Order Out of Chaos* by Ilya Prigogine. New York: Bantam Books.

Triplett, R. 1983. *Stage Fright, Letting It Work for You.* Chicago: Nelson-Hall.

Wiesel, E. 1982. Article in *New York Times,* October 13.

Wilson, F. 1986. *Tone Deaf and All Thumbs? An Invitation to Music-Making for Late Bloomers and Non-Prodigies.* New York: Viking Penguin, a division of Penguin Books USA, Inc.

Woolfolk, R. and Lehrer, P. 1984. *Principles and Practice of Stress Management.* New York: Guilford Press.